IF YOU ANSWER "YES" TO ANY OF
THESE QUESTIONS, DRU SCOTT'S UNIQUE
PROGRAM WILL HELP YOU PUT MORE
TIME IN YOUR LIFE:

—Do you want to be a star in the office without being a
workaholic?

—Do you want to take care of your house without letting
it be your prison?

—Do you want to relate in a giving way to loved ones
and friends without giving away too much of yourself
for your own good?

—Do you want to achieve both short-term and long-term
goals without mixing them up?

—Do you want to stop procrastinating, being late, feeling
one step behind and snowed under?

—Do you want to get on top of things and stay there?

If you want to, you can—with the one book that shows
you how to do it all with time to spare—

"An encouraging program that helps you define what you
want from life and offers practical steps to help you
achieve that goal."                    —Stephanie Winston
                                    author of *Getting Organized*

ABOUT THE AUTHOR:

DRU SCOTT, Ph.D., finds time to head her own
San Francisco-based management education firm,
travel and lecture extensively, appear in industrial
educational films, and author books, among them
her recent, acclaimed *Women as Winners*.

## SIGNET and MENTOR Books of Related Interest

# HOW TO PUT
# MORE
# TIME
## IN YOUR
# LIFE

## DRU SCOTT, Ph.D.

A SIGNET BOOK

**NEW AMERICAN LIBRARY**

TIMES MIRROR

*Dedicated to*
Elizabeth Paeth, M.D.
Wife of one
Mother of four
Manager of sixty
Physician for hundreds

Who adds so much to all the people in her life
through her everyday commitment to
quality and
timeless values.

# ACKNOWLEDGMENTS

With deep appreciation for the people who have participated in my seminars and speeches over the years. Without their shared experiences, probing questions, and thoughtful attention, this book would not have been possible.

With gratitude to the people whose ideas and inspirations have contributed so much to this book and to me.

Mary Butler
Peter Drucker
Ken Ernst, Ph.D.
Brenda Fanning Foster
Mary McClure Goulding, M.S.W.
Robert Goulding, M.D.
Stephen Karpman, M.D.
Sally Keen
Fredrick Lasker, M.D.
Abraham Maslow
James Morgan, Ph.D.
Joan Springer
Bep Van Beijmerwerdt
Paul Ware, M.D.

With grateful thanks to Theo Steele for fine editorial work and to Debra Smith who managed Dru Scott Associates, Inc. so capably while I took time off to write. Each brings a commitment to quality and the enjoyment of accomplishment to their work. Thanks also to Julie Rodenburg and Sandy McPartlon for their work in preparing the manuscript.

With appreciation to the Rawson, Wade staff for their support, and to Sharon Morgan for her work on this project.

With continuing gratitude to Eleanor Rawson for her wonderful encouragement to "Go ahead and do it now."

# PREFACE

Why I Wrote This Book

This book is different from any other book or film I've been involved with. When I first sat down to work on it, I knew that it was special—that it was a book I almost "had" to write.

The ideas in this book aren't static lessons that I have learned completely and can now forget. They are lessons that I will continue to relearn for the rest of my life, like favorite books that I reread a couple of times every year.

Some of the material about applying the ideas may seem very detailed. Remember that I'm writing for the tough case like myself—the person who is often most resistant to doing what is best for himself or herself (or myself).

Have you experienced the pain of wanting to do something, knowing it is the best thing to do, and then falling short? If you have, you particularly understand the exhilarating sense of relief and joy involved in mastering something that is important in your life. For most of my life, I dashed breathlessly from one panic or crisis to the next. Although I will not continue this kind of behavior, it is an old pattern that I'll always have to check, like those people who acquire fat cells as infants and must monitor their weight carefully for the rest of their lives. If, like me, you have ever spent an extended period of time in rushing, disorganization, or chaos, you know the comfort of having an easy, enjoyable ongoing program to help you achieve the quality of time you want in your life.

Writing this book has been a great opportunity for me to grow. I hope reading it will be great for you.

*Dru Scott*
*San Francisco*
*March 1980*

# CONTENTS

**PREFACE**

1. Reaching Beyond Time Management—The Promise
   of Quality                                                    *1*

### STEP 1. EXPLORE THE PSYCHOLOGY OF
### TIME—YOUR TIME MANAGEMENT STYLE 9

2. Exposing Myths About Time Management—Lifting
   the Veil                                                      *11*
3. The Secret Pleasures of Mismanaging Time                      *18*
4. Stimulation, Excitement, Defiance, and Your Time              *26*
5. The Guilt Trap—World Champion Time Waster                     *34*
6. What You Learned About Time from Mom and Dad                  *42*
7. Doing It Your Way—Add Style to Time
   Management                                                    *47*
8. Compulsive Time/Choice Time—Problem and
   Potential                                                     *51*
9. The Five Types of Compulsive Time                             *56*

### STEP 2. GET YOURSELF ORGANIZED
### AND GOING—IMPROVE YOUR LIFESTYLE
### AND ACCOMPLISHMENTS 65

10. How to Get Organized in Spite of Too Many
    Demands                                                      *67*
11. How to Set Objectives When You Don't Even Know
    What You Want                                                *75*
12. How to Set Priorities When There's Just Too Much
    to Do                                                        *83*
13. Speed Up Decisionmaking                                      *92*
14. Get into Gear and Keep Your System Running
    Smoothly                                                     *101*
15. A High-gear Program Needs the Right Equipment                *105*

### STEP 3. KEEP YOURSELF GOING—A PROGRAM FOR SELF-MOTIVATION *111*

16. Your Procrastination Profile  *113*
17. Procrastination Prevention  *117*
18. Emergency Care for a Bad Case of Procrastination  *125*


### STEP 4. COPE WITH EVERYDAY TIME DEMANDS—CREATIVE STRATEGIES *129*

19. When Mornings Are a Mess—Clean Up Your Act  *131*
20. Commute and Travel Time—Check Your Destination  *139*
21. Early Excitement Beats Running Late  *145*
22. Break Free of Time You Waste Waiting  *152*
23. Shopping and Housework—Programs Versus Projects  *157*
24. Exercise—Get Your Piece of "Pie"  *163*


### STEP 5. PUT YOUR TIME TO WORK— ON AND OFF THE JOB *167*

25. Paperwork—Feel Buried by the Avalanche?  *169*
26. Interruptions—Coping Without Being Rude  *179*
27. The Telephone—Tool or Tyrant  *183*
28. Are You a Workaholic?  *188*
29. Five Steps to Frustration-free Time with Your Boss  *193*
30. Make Your Meeting Time Count  *198*
31. "Yes" Is a Time Trap When You Want to Say "No"  *203*
32. Give Yourself the Gift of Time  *211*

REFERENCES AND READINGS  *213*

INDEX  *215*

# 1

# REACHING BEYOND TIME MANAGEMENT—
# THE PROMISE OF QUALITY

If you've ever yearned for an extra hour in your day, this book is for you. It won't mysteriously produce that twenty-fifth hour out of a magician's hat, but it will do something more realistic, more rewarding, and more lasting. This book will help you experience more time in your life through a commitment to *quality* time.

You will learn how to enhance the quality of your time to a degree you may never have dreamed possible. You can enrich your minutes, your hours, your days—your life.

You will learn how to make your time count in terms of what really matters. You will discover how to allow each moment to unfold and reveal all the color, richness, and satisfaction it holds for you.

You will learn how to achieve highly productive and energetic time, because you balance productive, purposeful time periods—"time in"—with equally important periods of total relaxation—"time out." The "time out" helps you recharge your batteries—a vital process if you want to be enthusiastic and effective during "time in."

You will learn specific and practical techniques to deal with nagging time problems. You will learn how to achieve your objectives faster, and you will discover some important psychological insights that will help you to move beyond the limitations of traditional time management.

## WHEN PEOPLE COMPLICATE YOUR TIME

The process of enriching and enhancing your time is not without complication. For most of us, learning how to use time to do what is most productive, healthy, and satisfying requires much more than the cold and impersonal techniques common to traditional time management. That's because time management does involve people . . . and people do compli-

1

cate our time. These traditional methods don't work for many people because they ignore a basic reality—we are not totally free of responsibilities to others. Most of us are not in a position to ignore others in our lives. We can't shut doors and closet ourselves for hours of uninterrupted planning. We have bosses, co-workers, customers, subordinates, spouses, children, friends, parents . . . all of whom make demands on our time. All of them to whom we have some responsibility.

Most of us are not willing to exploit every contact and every moment in selfish pursuit of our goals. We want more from our time, but we're also concerned with others' feelings. We want to be a cooperative team player, not a lone wolf. All this points to the need for personalized, creative time techniques that take people into consideration.

## THE SUCCESS FACTOR— WHY THIS PROGRAM WORKS

This people-oriented approach to time management is the first of four major reasons why my program will work for you when others may not have been enough.

The second reason is the program's lack of narrow and dictatorial "shoulds" and "musts." Most of us do not need any more scoldings or "musts" about time. This book does *not* prescribe one rigid set of rules for everyone to follow; it does provide stimulating and practical ideas to help you design and develop your *own* personal time management style.

Traditional time management focuses on accomplishments, yet *how* you live your life may be equally important to you. Not everyone is willing to sacrifice everything in life to become president of the company. For this reason we'll be considering both accomplishments *and* lifestyle.

The third reason why this book can help you is its emphasis on both information and motivation. It contains dozens of practical time management ideas, and spells out the motivational techniques you can use to implement the ideas. In other words, it covers *how you can get yourself to do what you already know you need to do*.

The fourth reason is the book's lack of technical terminology. Although I examine the psychological aspects of time use, I deliberately avoid using clinical psychological terms to explain the reasons that underlie many time management problems. Every profession has its own jargon. However, these handy but often half-understood labels can block a clear understanding of the real issues. Having a friend nod knowingly and label your behavior "obsessive compulsive" or "typical neurotic sense of inferiority" doesn't help. Such labels usually prevent you both from really understanding the issues and from taking constructive action.

## NO RIGID RULE BOOK

For the past ten years, my work in speaking and leading seminars, and as a psychologist, has taken me to many different parts of the country. I've been in touch with a wide variety of groups and individuals, including corporate directors, blue-collar supervisors, personnel counselors, sales managers and sales people, secretaries, and homemakers. Through these contacts, I have learned that many time management systems fail because they assume that there is one single answer for everyone's time problems. There isn't. There is a tremendous variety of individual needs and solutions.

Rather than attempting to impose one rigid set of rules for everyone to follow, this book will show you how to design a flexible program that's right for *you*. No one knows your pressures and problems as well as you do. That's why you are the best person to decide which of the techniques and ideas I will share with you will work best for you.

It is equally true that no one understands *your priorities* as well as you do. That's why this book will help you discover *what* really counts for you before concentrating on *how* to do anything. You will learn how to clarify your own individual values and central concerns.

Although there isn't just one answer, there are proven shortcuts to learning this psychologically based approach. You will be reaping benefits contributed by thousands of people I have worked with over the years. I am grateful to my clients for allowing me to discuss, experiment, and help them put together programs that enhance their own time management styles.

## INFORMATION AND MOTIVATION— THE WINNING COMBINATION

Time and again people tell me, "I know what to do. I just don't know how to get myself to do it." In situations like these, more information on time techniques isn't the solution.

No amount of information will solve a motivational problem. Few of us consistently do all the things we know we need to be doing—whether it's exercise, eating correctly, or financial planning. Most of us need to motivate ourselves much more effectively if we want to enhance the quality of our time.

I learned this lesson the hard way some years ago, and it is one of the main reasons why I wrote this book.

At that point in my career, I knew all the current theories in time management. I had even been successful in helping others learn to use their time more effectively. But one day I was brought up short by the realization that although I knew what to do, I wasn't doing all the things I needed to do in my own life. I needed something more. Here is how I gained that insight.

There were phones ringing, calls to return, a pile of letters begging to be answered, three people I just had to see immediately, weeks of expense records to catch up on. My desk was stacked high with paperwork. Looking at the ugly backlog just made the constantly nagging chorus in my mind grow louder, "You'll never make it. You'll never get caught up!"

My stress-tightened heart already felt the pressure of too many demands. The dull, aching tension in my neck and shoulders reminded me of my physician's parting words the day before: "You have high blood pressure—150 over 94—and you're barely thirty years old. You've got to slow down. You've got to do something different."

But my work was exciting and interesting, and I loved the freelance writing and consulting I was beginning to do. Later that day, as I raced through the park to an appointment with my publisher, my head kept throbbing. The thought kept pounding, "I can't go on like this. I know the time management techniques, I've taught them, written about them, but I need something more. I have all the information; why isn't it working for me?"

## A TURNING POINT

That was a painful moment for me, but it marked a turning point in my life. I decided that I deserved to live as well as I knew how. I was determined to find a way out, to discover a solution to my problem. What I learned are the self-motivation techniques that now form a vital part of my program.

I recall those times occasionally as I run leisurely along the ocean's edge, feeling lightness and movement in my shoulders. The satisfaction and joy of breathing cold, salty air provides a dramatic contrast to those days when I felt too pressured to take even one deep breath of stale office air.

Today I handle my time differently. Although my career is even more demanding, my blood pressure is normal. I learned that information was useless if I didn't motivate myself to act on that information.

You can use this two-pronged approach of information and motivation to enhance the quality of both your accomplishments and your lifestyle. Dozens of people I've talked to have accomplished great things, but they are unhappy with their general lifestyle. You can learn to achieve satisfaction in both these key areas.

## SUFFERING IS OVERRATED

Suffering rarely generates effective time use. More often, it hampers you. That's why I *won't* advise you to grit your teeth and forge ahead. I *will* provide lots of fascinating ideas and practical information that will help you motivate yourself to accomplish your objectives quickly and easily, and to enjoy your life more fully every day. When you learn how to put more quality time in your life, you can have both.

## THE THERAPEUTIC APPROACH TO TIME— HOW THIS BOOK IS ORGANIZED

This book employs a proven therapeutic approach that will provide immediate results. It focuses on specific problems and then relates them to general concepts. You can identify quickly with the problems and then learn their causes and cures. You can also multiply your benefits, because you can use the ideas to solve other problems.

Five major steps offer you the information you need to develop a flexible time program that will work for you.

Step One examines the psychology of time. It exposes some common myths about time, shows how you may be letting inappropriate guilt lock you into wasteful patterns, and uncovers the secret and sometimes surprising pleasures of mismanaging time. You will discover how childhood programming shapes adult behavior and time use. You'll learn how your own need for stimulation and excitement affects your use of time.

This step concludes with explicit strategies that help you

discover, design, and develop your own personal time management style.

Step Two demonstrates how to overcome pressures and procrastination, and use time management to improve your lifestyle and accomplishments. Even if you feel hopelessly disorganized and don't know what you want or where to begin, you'll learn how to take the first steps, and set objectives, assign priorities, overcome indecision, and conquer chronic worry. Subsequent chapters cover setting up a workable system and selecting the equipment that will make *your* system an ongoing success.

Step Three deals with the all-important subject of motivation. You will learn how to conquer procrastination and keep yourself going with a comprehensive program that incorporates your Stimulation and Excitement Quota, early unsatisfied needs, and the use of reinforcements and rewards.

Step Four tackles the time problems that many of us must cope with in our daily lives. It includes short, idea-packed chapters on creating a relaxed morning routine, reducing time lost in waiting or commuting, solving the lateness syndrome, organizing household chores, and setting up an enjoyable exercise program.

In Step Five, you will learn how to put your time to work on the job and in your social life. You'll learn how to handle annoying interruptions from friends and colleagues with tact and skill. You'll learn how to use the telephone effectively, how to say "No" when you really want to, how to reduce mountains of paperwork, and how to get the most from your time at meetings and with your boss.

## THE UNDERLYING THEMES

Although there are dozens of ideas in this book, you don't need to learn them all to achieve the quality of time you want. You only need to use a few techniques that best fit your own personality, problems, and situation.

Whichever techniques you select, however, you'll discover they all relate to the three major themes in this book:

    I. *Clarify priorities for yourself and others*
- Concentrate on quality.
- Fulfill wants and objectives.
- Define and do what really counts right now.

    II. *Understand motivations*

- Face up to mixed feelings in yourself and others.
- Reward and reinforce the best in yourself and others.
- Motivate yourself to do what you most want—every day.

III. *Do your best with this day*
- Don't wait to live fully.
- Open yourself to the joys of this moment.
- Go ahead, do it. The best is now.

## MORE THAN MEETS THE EYE— HOW TO USE THIS BOOK

Consider this book as a resource—its ideas will have lasting value. It will provide you with the information you need to build and maintain a personalized time program that will shelter and protect the lifestyle you want. There's also a vital plus to this book. A deeper understanding of the psychological and motivational side of time management is the "something more" that makes the difference. It means freedom to live your life fully every moment.

This book is packed with ideas that will stimulate your own insights, and you'll want to jot many down. You will also find exercises that will reveal a fresh perspective on your use of time. So get yourself a notebook right now and use it to collect all the material you need as you read the book: the exercises, the techniques you select, the insights that hit closest to home, the creative ideas that occur to you. Don't put a stopper on your imagination. You will probably come up with original techniques of your own. Use your notebook as a personal reference. By the time you finish this book, you'll have created a blueprint for your own time management program.

You may be tempted to feel, "This program can't work for me. You don't know my boss, my organization, my family, my . . ." Stop a moment. The fact that you are reading this book right now means your interest level is high. You know you want to accomplish even more, in spite of all the people complications. You know you want more from your time, to enjoy every day fully. Couple your desires with the exciting ideas in this book. You'll have a winning combination. Today is the best day to put even more quality time in your life.

# *Step 1.*
## Explore
## the Psychology
## of Time

---

## Your Time
## Management Style

# 2

## EXPOSING MYTHS ABOUT
## TIME MANAGEMENT—
## LIFTING THE VEIL

Many of us feel helpless when we think about improving our use of time because we unknowingly rely on inaccurate assumptions. These assumptions are so common that we accept them without ever questioning their validity. However, if you examine these assumptions in the light of today's reality, they reveal themselves for what they are—mere myths.

Here are ten of the most common myths about time management. Take a good look at them all. Are any of them assumptions you've unconsciously accepted? If they are, you are letting them hamper your freedom to get what you want and need from your time. They need to be cleared away.

### MYTH NO. 1:
### "I'M WAITING UNTIL I HAVE MORE TIME"

This is a very common myth. Consider it logically and you'll realize it doesn't hold up. Putting off doing what counts most to you now until you have "more time" is like saying that you can't go on a diet until you lose some weight.

Many of us let ourselves slide into believing that *someday*—when the kids grow up, when the mortgage is paid off, when we have a better job, when a new relationship develops—something different will happen. Suddenly we'll have more time to do what we want or need to do. This passive "waiting until" attitude allows precious time to slip through our fingers like water, to disappear forever.

"I'm waiting until I have more time" is not an accurate statement of reality. It's an outmoded state of mind. A colleague of mine realized this one day when she visited her eighty-seven-year-old aunt in a retirement home. It was just two days before Christmas and my friend was caught up in her usual last-minute holiday rush. As she drove to the retirement community, she reflected that one benefit of retirement

11

would be a greater amount of free time to do the things she felt her busy life now kept her from doing.

The scene at the retirement home put an end to that myth. Five residents waited impatiently in the hall for a mini-bus that would take them to town for some last-minute holiday errands. A woman went whizzing by in her motorized wheelchair, muttering that she'd never get all her cards in the mail on time. A member of the decoration committee was explaining that she hadn't time to order the new Christmas tree lights. To cap it all, my colleague's aunt came breathlessly to meet her, complaining that she still hadn't finished making all her presents for the family.

At that moment, my friend realized that no matter how long she waited, she'd never have that mythical state of "more time" dropped in her lap.

Accept the reality of the twenty-four-hour day. Invest your energies in getting the most out of *this* moment, not in futile waiting "until."

## MYTH NO. 2: "IT DOESN'T WORK FOR ME"

If you've made this statement in the past, take a minute to examine how you use this expression. It's accurate to say that some time techniques may not meet your needs. If this is the case, put those techniques aside and select others that do.

If, on the other hand, this statement conveys a hidden hope that the technique alone will do the job for you, reconsider. A workbench full of tools is useless without a pair of hands to do the work. Time techniques are only tools; they can help make our work easier, but they can't do the job by themselves. Their degree of usefulness depends on the skill with which we use them. We sharpen our skills when we use them again and again. They are most beneficial when we integrate them into our everyday style of time management.

Select your time techniques wisely. Experiment to find the ones that work best for you. Develop your skill in using them. Put them to work for you on a continuing basis. If you use the expression, "It won't work for me," use it accurately.

## MYTH NO. 3: "I ALWAYS LOSE MY LIST"

Most of us don't realize how complex we are. Our needs and desires are often in flux, and sometimes actually in direct opposition to each other. Everyone has mixed feelings at one time or another. Part of a person may sincerely, even desperately, want to manage time better. Another facet of that same person may fear the changes that smoother operation could bring. As soon as that person has written a well-intentioned "to do" list, another facet accidentally tucks it into some out-of-the-way corner.

This *isn't* schizophrenic. It simply reveals how complex and intricate we all are. Conflicting feelings are common human behavior.

Betsy F., a habitual list-loser, found a creative way to solve her problem. "Accepting that I both loved and hated my 'Must Do' lists gave me an entirely new perspective," she told me. "I wanted to get things done, but every time I saw those words, 'Must Do,' at the top of my daily list I felt nagged. I was always losing my list, scolding myself for losing it, taking more time to write out another list—and then losing that one, too! I solved my problem when I changed the title of the list. Now I write a list of 'Potential Accomplishments' each day and hang it right by the telephone. I haven't lost one since," she concluded with a smile.

Although list-losing may be one of your time problems, Betsy F.'s particular solution may not be the best one for you. The important thing to remember is that we all have mixed feelings. Recognize them and accept them as part of the human condition. If you lose lists continually, analyze your feelings and find out why. Work out a creative solution acceptable to all the facets of your own personality.

## MYTH NO. 4:
### "BUT I'VE ALREADY TAKEN *THE* TIME MANAGEMENT COURSE OR READ *THE* BOOK"

Most people who use their time well are continually looking for new techniques or new ways to apply old techniques. They investigate all available resources, get the best information they can, then choose the techniques that are right for their needs. They know the key is to use the techniques frequently, and incorporate them into the daily routine.

Time management is not a "once only" get-organized project, it's an ongoing program to bring order into their lives. You have never eaten a meal so nourishing that you don't have to eat again. You have to refill the gas tank periodically if you want to keep driving your car. Just as there are no one-time meals or one-fill gas tanks, there are no one-time courses or books.

Booster shots are more effective than a one-time inoculation. Read all the books you can get your hands on. Take the courses, listen to tapes, talk to other people. Keep yourself well supplied with ideas and inspiration. It's the best way to keep yourself on target with your time.

### MYTH NO. 5: "YOU JUST CAN'T GET ORGANIZED AROUND HERE"

There's no question about it—it is easier to get organized when the people around you use their time well. That's one reason why it pays off to help others improve their use of time. But don't let an imperfect situation be an excuse to do *nothing* about your own time problems. Resentment about the disorganization around you is a waste of your time. Take the initiative. Work on improving your own time use. Do what you can, regardless of less-than-ideal circumstances.

Let the people around you know you are working to improve your time use. Respect the fact that some of them have rough situations. Some may not believe that time management can make a difference. Don't focus on their disorganization. Instead, ask them how you can make your time together more productive. Your questions may help them see their own time problems in a new light, and provide the inspiration they need. Even if you can't create an ideal situation, you will be getting more from your own time. That alone can lead to an appreciable improvement in your situation.

### MYTH NO. 6: "BUT THERE'S *NOTHING* I CAN DO"

If you find yourself making this statement, you may be reacting to a pressure-packed situation. It may describe your feelings of being overwhelmed, but it's not an accurate statement of your time management capabilities. You may not always be able to do *everything* you would like to do or need to do, but you can certainly take some preliminary steps. A compromise tactic can provide you with a solution.

For example, you may need a full eight hours to write a tough report, but that block of time simply may not be available. Don't let that stop you from taking some action. Carve out a half hour each day to work on the report. It's not ideal, but it adds up and it will help. At the very least, it will allay those feelings of being swamped, and put *you* back in control of the situation.

## MYTH NO. 7:
### "PEOPLE KEEP INTERRUPTING ME"

For most of us, interruptions are a big problem. We all may long to lock ourselves safely away from all interruptions, but we rarely achieve that blissful state. Waiting for it to materialize before you begin to get a better handle on your time is as fruitless as waiting for that mythical twenty-five-hour day. Interruptions are an inevitable part of everyday living. Don't waste time waiting for them to disappear. Learn how to handle them instead. It's vital to successful time management.

Chapters 10 and 26 will show you how to get what you want and need from your time in spite of interruptions. You can learn how to deal with them courteously, considerately, and creatively. Whether you have two toddlers underfoot or an office full of talkative co-workers, you can learn techniques that will free you from unnecessary interruptions.

## MYTH NO. 8:
### "TIME MANAGEMENT IS BORING"

Traditional time management can be dull. Many of us aren't willing to suffer the boredom even though we really do want to be more productive. Those last-minute rushes are exciting, and there is an intense thrill in handling a crisis. We may pay a high price for this excitement, but at least we're not bored.

If you have not explored time management techniques because they are boring, I have good news. You can get what you want 'from your time and still keep it as stimulating and exciting as you want it to be. Making time management effective *and* exciting is the revolutionary thrust of this book.

## MYTH NO. 9: "ISN'T THERE A DANGER YOU'LL GET SO ORGANIZED YOU CAN'T GET ANYTHING DONE?"

There's often a hidden fear behind this concern—the fear that someone or something will control you. Therefore, it is crucial to understand that time techniques *cannot* control you. *You* are in charge of *them*. They are only a passive collection of tools that you can use in any way you wish. You are the one who is in control of your time.

If you express this concern, I know that you are already aware of the danger of becoming a "list and schedule fanatic"—someone who makes dozens of lists but gets nothing done. You don't have to worry. You are not the kind of person who will spend so much time getting organized that you can't get anything done.

### MYTH NO. 10:
### "I NEED SOMEONE TO MOTIVATE ME"

This myth is as old as the hills. It's based on the common belief that someone or something outside ourselves controls our feelings. The idea crops up in hundreds of common expressions; "You make me angry," and "You make me happy," are two prime examples. Although they are common, they aren't accurate. We may feel angry about a particular incident or a colleague's behavior, but that person or event does not have the power to *make* us angry. We may feel happy when we hear a lovely song or see someone we admire, but that song or person doesn't *make* us happy. It's a fine distinction, but an important one. The reality is that we are all in charge of our own feelings. The language in this book was carefully selected to reinforce that reality. You won't read that anger sets up a barrier to good time management. You will read that *you* may delay solving time problems, when you are angry. You are in charge of your own feelings. You don't have to wait for anyone else to inspire you. You can be your own inspiration.

### CLEAR OUT OLD MYTHS—
### GIVE YOURSELF A FRESH START

If any of these myths sounds familiar, keep your ears open. When you hear yourself or someone else make one of these statements, remember what you've learned in this chapter:

- Myths are nothing more than stumbling blocks.
- Don't allow them to block you from experiencing the richness and diversity of every moment of your life.
- Understand how these myths encourage you to hold

yourself back from getting what you most want from your time.

- Clear out these old myths and give yourself a fresh start. You'll free yourself to begin the exciting process of putting more time in your life.

# 3

# THE SECRET PLEASURES
# OF MISMANAGING TIME

You may be all too familiar with the many problems that mismanaging time can stir up. Did you ever realize that it offers secret pleasures as well? Without being aware of it, you may already have a clue to what they are. You may even have experienced some of them yourself.

Have you ever put off an important project until the last minute—even when you could have done it earlier? Ever made a wild and frantic dash to get to an appointment you could have left for earlier? Have you ever known an activity was off target and heading you straight for a time crunch—and you still kept at it? Those last-minute crunches are charged with electricity, aren't they?

Mismanaging time can pay off in some rarely revealed ways that many of us unconsciously take advantage of. Some of us mismanage time to get attention or gain a sense of power. Mismanaging time also can serve as a way to avoid unpleasant tasks or shirk personal responsibility. It can be used to resist change, sidestep new feelings, avoid feeling close to others, and deal with that age-old fear of feeling "too good."

However, don't make a blanket indictment of the time mismanagement practices this chapter will reveal. We all gain something from our use of time, even when we mismanage it. But it is important to understand what the secret payoffs are. Uncovering hidden or conflicting motivations gives you a handle on this information. When you understand motivations, you work more effectively with the people around you. You are also equipped to make wiser decisions about your own time. You don't have to change your behavior just because you've learned about these secret payoffs, but if you decide you want to, you can do it faster and more easily.

## GETTING ATTENTION—
## "LOOK, MA! NO HANDS!"

In today's crowded, rushed, and anonymous world, it's hard to dream up any sure-fire techniques for being noticed. Time mismanagement has emerged as one of the few proven attention-getters.

Picture the people in your life who don't handle their time well. It's highly probable that this behavior gets them a lot of attention. Relatives nag them, co-workers chide them, friends schedule plans around them. People kid them about it. Sometimes the attention leaves a bad taste in their mouths; it's not always complimentary or admiring. But it *is* attention. Mismanaging their time gets them noticed.

Sally R. makes herself the center of attention at all staff meetings—regularly scheduled meetings, special project meetings, even emergency meetings. She always arrives late, bursting in with breathless apologies. She drops a load of charts and notes on the table, and pushes past everyone to get to the coatrack in the back of the room. She rattles the metal coathangers, apologizing again for the interruption. Then she offers a string of loudly whispered "Excuse me's" as she wriggles through the group to get to her seat. Although the other staff members are familiar with her antics, she is always noticed. She captures everyone's attention—and their time.

The late-arrival technique has many variations, but it's always an attention-getter. Surely you've run into someone who arrives late at every party to make a "grand entrance." What about the dinner guest who is chronically late? All the other guests have been there for an hour. They've munched through the hors d'oeuvres, had a couple of drinks, made inroads on the salted peanuts. They want to sit down to dinner. Delicious aromas waft from the kitchen, and the hostess is beginning to worry that the veal will be overcooked. The host wonders if he should offer another round of drinks. Then in sails the latecomer, full of excuses. Everyone is so happy they can finally eat that, instead of being greeted angrily, he or she is welcomed with enthusiasm and relief.

Arriving late is an old and common way to get attention. Those who make it a practice may be reluctant to give it up until they find something that works just as well. In subsequent chapters, you'll discover a variety of ways that such people can learn to get the recognition they want and deserve without imposing unfairly on others.

## SECRET POWER—
## "I'LL SHOW YOU WHO'S BOSS!"

Many people feel powerless to control their own destiny in our modern mass society. Some react by trying to gain control in a variety of everyday situations. For example, on her way out to lunch with a group of friends, Myra decides that she must redo her makeup. The others shift around in the hall waiting for her, looking at their watches, and calculating whether they will get to the restaurant on time. Myra gains control by making them wait.

A major aspect of control is determining *when*. If the data-processing department delays the start of a marketing campaign because forecasts are late, data processing is in control. If a subordinate holds up the new project plans because he hasn't finished the graphics, unconsciously he is showing everyone who's boss. He also may risk planting the suspicion that he's inefficient, but for the moment, he gains a sense of control. If a low-ranking civilian guard on a military base stops every entering vehicle to make a maddeningly meticulous examination of passes, he's in control. A long line of colonels and captains may fume as they sit in their cars, but the guard controls the slow-moving line. This kind of control may only offer a *false* sense of power, but it is one of the ways mismanaging time can pay off.

## SIDESTEPPING THE UNPLEASANT—
## TOO BUSY TO TAKE OUT THE GARBAGE

Another reward of mismanaged time is the excuse to avoid some unpleasant duty.

A personnel director of a large corporation told me, "I know that one of our section heads needs to talk to one of his employees about her body odor. Customers even mention it. Whenever I ask him about it, he always tells me that he knows it's important but he hasn't had time. He's been putting off this unpleasant chore for six months because he's been 'running behind.' "

One dedicated volunteer in our community hates housework. She keeps so busy raising funds for charities and canvassing the neighborhood for political campaigns that she has no time to attack the muddy paw prints on the carpet or the grime in the bathroom.

A father who immerses himself completely in the demands of his work may feel totally justified in doing no housework, ignoring the dirty storm drains, or refusing to face the reality that one of his teenage children has a potential drug problem.

If everyone in the department knows that Jim never catches up on his workload, he won't receive extra responsibilities. When a difficult project comes up, it's given to someone else.

Running behind is a common excuse for putting off something that is hard to face. People even use it to avoid doing anything unpleasant at all.

## AVOIDING NEW FEELINGS— DON'T ROCK THE BOAT

Mismanaging time is an effective way to avoid certain emotions or self-evaluations. The emotions may be painful—feelings of rejection, awkwardness, or failure; they can also be pleasant feelings—acceptance and love for who we are, intimacy with someone we love, success. Although it is hard to believe that someone would want to avoid such emotions, the unfamiliar can often be frightening.

A hardworking young executive assistant constantly talks about taking a disco dance class at the local community college to expand her social life. Each term, however, she's "just too busy" to sign up. Unconsciously, she's afraid she'll feel awkward or clumsy when she's learning the dance steps, or opening conversations with strangers. So she spends her evenings reading instead of making the new friends she wants.

A college professor puts off completing his novel. He's too busy making the lesson plans. Although he's not aware of it, he fears becoming a successful novelist. His parents were working-class people who never completed high school. The status of a college professor is a dizzying one by comparison. If he were to become a celebrated novelist on top of that, he is afraid he might be in over his head. The lesson plans get written; his novel doesn't.

Sales people who procrastinate and develop "call reluctance" are usually fending off feelings of rejection. If you want to ask someone out to dinner but keep putting it off, it could be for the same reason. You might have an enjoyable date, but you don't want to risk rejection.

Some people feel that their work is the only justification for their existence. They hide themselves in busy work because they fear the unfamiliar feelings of being loved and accepted for *who they are,* not just for what they do.

Most of us have mixed emotions about new situations and new feelings. A part of us may desperately want to feel successful, loved, accepted, positive about ourselves and our lives. Another part may find it's not always easy to embrace new feelings. It can be difficult to let go of the familiar, even when it's painful.

### SHIRKING PERSONAL RESPONSIBILITY— "WHY DIDN'T YOU REMIND ME?"

Time mismanagement can serve as a handy excuse for sidestepping personal responsibility.

- A teenager misses his appointment at the orthodontist and blusters to his mother, "You're supposed to keep track of dates. Why didn't you remind me?"
- A defensive husband wails to his wife, "You know I wanted to get you an anniversary present. Why didn't you tell me it was today?"
- A woman driving her children to a mountain campsite fumes when they run out of gas on a lonely road, "I can't keep my eyes on the gas gauge when I'm driving. Why didn't you remind me to get gas in that last town?"

Some people continually mismanage their time to avoid accepting responsibility. They want somebody else to do the job for them.

Sandy J. blithely tells everyone that she never wears a watch. She's really saying, "It's *your* responsibility to make sure I get where I'm going on time."

A personnel director I worked with recognized that a number of employees at her company used this ploy. They'd beg her to set up training programs, but unless she reminded them constantly, they'd "forget" to show up.

Tossing responsibility to someone else isn't a payoff that many people are aware they get from mismanaging their time. Keep your ears open, though. You'll be surprised at how often you hear, "Why didn't you remind me?"

## RESISTING CHANGE—
## "I'VE ALWAYS DONE IT THIS WAY"

People resist change largely because familiar ways of doing things have become comfortable habits. They are like the big, old, comfortable armchair a friend's grandfather refused to give up. The upholstery was faded, the stuffing was coming out of the cushions, and the springs were useless, but he refused to get a new one.

"That old chair is comfortable," he affirmed stoutly. "Sitting in something new to read the paper wouldn't seem natural."

If time mismanagement has become a comfortable old habit, it, too, will feel "natural." You may resist a more pleasurable and productive method because it feels strange and unnatural at first. You may hang on to the old habit even it if is no longer useful.

An executive who was once the best typist in the secretarial pool has this problem. When her secretary produces a letter with typos, she retypes it herself. "It saves time," she says. In the long run it would save more time to teach the secretary accuracy.

Susan P. was so busy that she never had any time to plan ahead. She worked out a way to overcome her tendency to cling to this old habit. She sat down with her children and explained that she wanted a half hour every evening to plan the next day's activities.

"At first, it didn't seem natural to any of us, least of all me," she reported. "I didn't feel comfortable shutting myself away from the children like that. But they learned to leave me alone, and I put my thoughts in order. The planning I do gives all our lives a boost."

## FEAR OF FEELING "TOO GOOD"—
## WAITING FOR THE OTHER SHOE TO DROP

Many people mismanage their time because of a fear that's as old as history. It's the illogical but very common feeling that if things are going too smoothly, fate will intervene. Something bad is bound to happen. They don't want to risk that, so they *mis*manage their time—it's a kind of hex-insurance.

Many of us also have absorbed the Puritan concept that there's something sinful about enjoyment. If we have too much fun, punishment lurks around the corner. If it feels good, then it must be either fattening, sinful, or carcinogenic.

When you manage your time well, you feel good and enjoy life more. If you're afraid of feeling too good, you have an excellent reason to avoid putting your life in order; you gain too much from your inefficient use of time.

Forestalling the possibility of feeling good may seem like a negative payoff, but it is one of the most common reasons why people don't use their time skillfully. You can overcome this outdated fear by continually reinforcing your trust in joy.

## AVOIDING CLOSENESS—
## KEEP YOUR DISTANCE

Another deep-seated reason for the mismanagement of time is the fear of closeness. Unknowingly, we may set ourselves up to avoid the opportunity for intimacy—even with those we love.

One business man literally built a wall between himself and his wife with his briefcase. As she sat across from him at the table after dinner, he'd flip through folders with one hand and tap out monthly sales figures on a calculator with the other. She saw more of his briefcase than she did of him. There was no opportunity for intimate conversation.

A recently divorced woman confessed that she now realized she had used an endless supply of chores like armor. She never had time to talk with her husband about his problems. When she did listen, she was always attending to something else—cataloging the slides from last year's vacation, sorting the children's laundry, balancing the checkbook. She said the marriage didn't explode all at once. It just slowly came apart at the seams.

Even in the act of seeking closeness, some of us find ways to avoid it. Consider the dating couple who plan an intimate evening of theater and dining. Neither makes a reservation at a restaurant. They spend their first twenty minutes deciding where to eat, then another ten minutes trying to book a table. When they are finally seated, they are hungry and irritable. There's no time left to savor the food. They must bolt it down if they are to get to the theater by curtain time. They lose the pleasure of a good dinner and each other's company. Then they dash to the theater and sit through the program feeling anything but close. More likely, they feel vaguely dissatisfied and somewhat pained by indigestion.

## THE SECRET IS OUT—
## BUT MUST YOU CHANGE?

- You don't necessarily have to change your behavior— you can go right on making those late-arrival "grand entrances" at parties if you want to. It's *your* choice.
- We all use our time to get something. It may be what we feel we need at the moment, or it may be something we needed in the past. Understand what it is. Face up to mixed feelings in yourself and others.
- When you understand conflicting motivations, you don't have to change anything—but you'll have an easier time making changes if that's what you decide to do.
- Change requires courage and determination. It holds the threat as well as the thrill of the unknown. When Shakespeare's Hamlet observes that we prefer to "bear those ills we have than fly to others that we know not of," he sums things up more poetically than a psychology textbook, but the idea is the same.
- Don't give up old ways of mismanaging time until you are ready to risk the rewards of greeting life with open arms, willing to accept the challenge, growth, and richness it offers.

# 4

# STIMULATION, EXCITEMENT, DEFIANCE, AND YOUR TIME

*E*very human being needs stimulation to survive. That's a proven psychological fact. Without attention, recognition, and contact, we can wither on the vine like a flower denied access to light and water. In addition, many of us need a more intense form of stimulation—we need excitement.

## THE EXCITEMENT OF THE LAST-MINUTE RUSH

A father of five regularly packs everyone and the family dog into the stationwagon for a Sunday drive in the country. Once or twice a month he delays stopping for gas until the tank is dangerously close to empty. They career down the road, craning their necks to spot an open service station. The air crackles with excitement. The anxiety level is high. The dog is barking. The children cheer as they finally pull into a station. They usually make it "in spite of," but the negative excitement generates tension they'd be happier without.

## DIFFERENT STIMULATION AND EXCITEMENT QUOTAS

We all have our own individual Stimulation and Excitement Quota. How we fill it affects our time. We get what we need in different ways. An elderly widow adds a dash of excitement to her quiet life with a last-minute flurry of arrangements for her monthly bridge party. A Broadway star dashes in just before curtain time and throws dozens of people into an uproar every night as they breathlessly help her get ready for the performance. One requires relatively little stimulation and excitement, the other a great deal.

We all fill our quota, whether we do it knowingly or unknowingly, positively or negatively. However, negative stimulation and excitement can produce harmful stress. Negative excitement doesn't come cheap. It takes a heavy toll emotionally and physically—on ourselves and others.

Let's probe into the hidden psychological reasons why some of us seek negative stimulation and excitement, and explore ways we can change that by filling out quotas positively. I will show you, as I have shown many others in my workshops, how to maintain the level of stimulation and excitement you need by being productive rather than destructive.

## FILLING A TEMPORARY VOID

Sometimes, people seek negative stimulation because of a temporary lack in positive stimulation. That's what led Carole H. into a situation that could have hurt her career.

Carole was one of the few women at her level of management in a major utilities company. Her boss took pride in pointing this out. He continually encouraged her and gave her work high visibility. Carole thrived until a new manager took over.

The new manager believed in a "leave them alone" leadership style. He rarely talked with Carole about work in progress. He was sparing in praise. After four months of this treatment, Carole found herself missing deadlines. For the first time in her life, she was leaving work until the last minute. She hated the stress, but didn't know why she was creating the situation. Her boss nagged her. She scolded herself. Things just got worse; she fell farther and farther behind. When Carole talked to me about her problem, I pointed out that at least she was getting attention. The light dawned. Carole realized the root of her problem.

Now Carole makes sure she gets the positive attention she needs to do a good job. She's developed a support group among her peers and people in other departments. They understand her work. They are delighted when she calls to tell them about a new accomplishment. She keeps her Stimulation and Excitement Quota on "full" from these sources. She respects her manager's style, but she also respects her own needs.

Stimulation is a basic need, one we all share. It doesn't show lack of maturity to seek it. Healthy human beings recognize the need. They learn how to take care of it productively.

## GETTING EVERYBODY INTO THE ACT

Some of us can get our stimulation privately. We can give ourselves a pat on the back, add zest to the day by taking a walk in the woods, derive excitement from planning a birthday surprise for someone we love. For those with a higher excitement level, private stimulation often isn't enough. Many need a barrage of crises to generate the intense excitement they require. They ignite excitement all around them, pulling others into the crisis with them.

A politician has a major address scheduled months in advance. His staff does all the backup work, but can never get him to sit down and hammer out the final speech. Somehow, something always gets in the way. The day before the event, he involves all of them in a twenty-four-hour speech-writing marathon. The crisis generates the excitement he needs to be "up" for his appearance. He makes a brilliant presentation. But his staff is drained, exhausted, left to pick up the pieces.

Negative excitement can extract a high toll from others. Eventually, the support troops may decide it's not worth it.

## DEEPER ROOTS OF DEFIANCE

People who habitually seek negative stimulation are often reacting to drives that stem from childhood patterns of defiance. *Defiance is a habitual reaction against perceived authority.* There are many degrees of defiance. Most successful sales people, lawyers, and entrepreneurs are defiant.

These patterns evolve from three basic decisions: "I'll show 'em," "You can't make me," and "I'll do it my way." Whether in response to spoken or nonverbal communication, they are the child's way of coping with messages that seem to say, "You'll never make it," or "You must do it my way," or "You can't do it."

A little girl reacts to her father's suggestion that she wear an angel costume to the kindergarten Halloween party by insisting she wants to be a witch instead. She wants to do it her way. A boy doesn't rebel openly when his mother calls, "Come in for dinner now." He just responds, "In a minute," and drags that minute out as long as he can. He's showing her that she can't make him. A child whose older brothers tell him he's too clumsy to join the baseball team defiantly practices batting at odd hours until he's good enough to hit home runs consistently.

An early decision to "show 'em" is often the key to survival for a young child. He or she resolves to make it *in spite of* all obstacles.

Later in life, some may continue to react this way. Even when it's not appropriate or helpful, they make every project a struggle. They feel they have to "prove" something.

### THE STRUGGLE AGAINST STRUCTURE— LISTS, CALENDARS, AND DEADLINES

People who exhibit defiant behavior continually struggle against structure in their lives. They view lists, calendars, and deadlines as objects to defy. They lose lists constantly, and can't take the time to keep a calendar. When they have a deadline, they rarely meet it. Even if they set the deadline themselves, they don't see it as something to be met. Unconsciously, they perceive it as one more opportunity to "show 'em," to succeed "in spite of." They aren't aware of it, but they are so used to overcoming obstacles that they create them even when they don't exist.

People who habitually react with defiance will move mountains to overcome an "insurmountable" obstacle. But they'll yawn when faced with an important task that seems too easy. They're bored. Even if the result is desirable, they aren't interested. Grabbing for the challenge is what triggers their enthusiasm.

### "JUST ONE MORE THING"— A COMMON PROCRASTINATION PLOY

Defiant behavior also turns up in a very common form of procrastination. It's the "Just One More Thing" syndrome. People caught up in this habit always feel they must do "just one more thing," even if it will make them late. A salesman who gets himself all set to leave the office on time for an important client meeting turns back at the door to make "just one more phone call." A lawyer on the way to catch a plane feels compelled to delay her departure by dictating "just one more memo." They get negative stimulation from this form of procrastination. It automatically creates a need for that exciting last-minute rush.

## THE DOUBLE BIND—
## CONFLICTING MOTIVATIONS

People who fervently want to improve their time use but fight suggested time techniques often feel trapped by old habits of defiance. I ran into a classic example of this in one of my time management seminars. A securities sales representative demonstrated strong motivation by enrolling in the seminar. He emphasized how much he wanted to improve his use of time. Yet each concept presented brought forth an objection. He'd say, "Wait a minute, it's not that easy," or "Are you trying to tell me . . . ?" Part of him wanted to improve his time use, yet another part kept digging up reasons why he couldn't. He made himself a prisoner of defiance, locked in painful conflict.

## A POSSIBLE PLUS

There's no doubt that an "I'll show 'em" reaction offers some rewards. The determination to overcome obstacles can contribute to success in a competitive society like ours. Defiant people refuse to accept temporary defeats. They struggle eternally against the odds, real or artificially produced. They develop a kind of energy and stamina that adds an edge in many situations.

## THE DARKER SIDE OF DEFIANCE

Despite the rewards it can offer, defiant behavior has a darker side. It usually involves "cutting off your nose to spite your face." It can set up rigid behavior patterns. When every aspect of life is seen as a contest, many avenues of growth and feeling are cut off. Personal fulfillment is blocked. This type of behavior is enormously wasteful in terms of human potential. It can rob you of quality time in some of the most important areas of your life.

If the roots of defiant behavior are deep, overnight change is unlikely. I have found psychotherapy that helps heal defiance well worth the time and money.

If you have a defiance problem, you can begin to work on it by substituting positive behavior that will fill your Stimulation and Excitement Quota more creatively. The change is well worth the effort. It's a relief to know you don't always have to struggle or suffer to pay for good times and good feelings. It's good to know you don't ever have to do anything to hurt yourself.

## FILL YOUR QUOTA CREATIVELY

When you understand why you seek negative stimulation and excitement, it is easier to create ways to fill your quota positively. The following case illustrates how one man did it.

Len A. confessed to having more than forty years' practice in defiant behavior. The long habits of constant struggle and last-minute rushes kept his Stimulation and Excitement Quota filled. The toll was high, however, and he wanted to find a better way. He realized he needed a lot of excitement, so he decided to discover positive ways to get it.

One Sunday afternoon Len sat down with a pot of coffee and a lined yellow pad. An hour later, he'd created a blueprint for satisfying his needs more creatively. Here's what his list contained:

1. Put at least one exciting activity on the calendar every day.
2. Use outside resources to help expand ideas for solving business problems—investment bankers, other financial officers, consultants, data research services, books and articles.
3. Do some work at different levels and in different areas to provide variety—spend some time in conceptual planning, some in people managing, some in a detail project, some on manual work like building bookshelves for the study.
4. Vary outside activities to include involvement with people in all walks of life—volunteer for the community fund drive, attend a city council meeting, join a church group, sign up as a Boy Scout troop leader.
5. Schedule time regularly with the children, individually and all together—take Eric to a football game, Margie to the Saturday matinee, Ellen to field hockey, all of them for a picnic at the beach.
6. Have an active and varied social life—spend some time with one person, some in groups; set aside time for both structured and unstructured activities.
7. Book interesting things ahead—subscribe to the sym-

phony series, get football season tickets, make reservations for that nightclub comic who's coming to town.

This list was only the beginning for Len, but it put him on the right track. He realized that only by substituting positive stimulation and excitement could he wean himself away from those old negative behavior patterns he wanted to change. Your Stimulation and Excitement Quota may be lower than Len's—or higher. Whatever the level, you can use a similar approach to fill it creatively and positively.

## YOU HAVE A CHOICE

What can you do if someone you are involved with has time problems that stem from defiance? It helps to understand that their actions aren't deliberate. But you don't have to suffer because of their unintentional behavior.

Take a good look at the benefits you get from the relationship, and consider what it costs you. Think about the costs and benefits involved for the other person. Understand the dynamics of his or her unproductive behavior, and don't reward and reinforce it. You can relate to that person constructively, and still take care of yourself.

George G. has been happily married for fifteen years to Sheila, a woman notorious for being late. He told me how he learned to live with her time habits:

"Sheila is an admirable woman in many ways. I delight in her company. I realized years ago, however, that I'd have to find a way to work around her time problems. I developed some guidelines that give me a backup plan. I don't let her lateness throw me into a turmoil.

"When Sheila and I set a specific time to meet, I know she'll usually be at least twenty minutes late. She always has some explanation. Most often, it's that she had to do one more thing before leaving. I used to wait on street corners. I'd stand there breathing in traffic fumes and building up an avalanche of anger waiting for her to arrive. I'd be so irritated, I wouldn't enjoy the first hour of our time together. Over the years, I learned this never helped.

"Now I always select some place where I won't mind waiting. Sometimes I choose an interesting hotel lobby, where I can watch the people going by. Other times, I pick a favorite restaurant. I can sit over a drink or contemplate the menu until Sheila shows up."

If you're involved in a similar situation, be realistic. Give yourself a backup plan. Figure out ways to make that waiting time enjoyable. Focus on what is important to *you* in the relationship, and move the other person's time problems to the periphery. They may not change their old habits, but you *can* find a way to do what is best for your time. The choice is yours. The time is yours.

## KEEP A CLEAR PERSPECTIVE

- Every human being needs stimulation and excitement to survive. It is a sign of maturity to recognize this need and take care of it.
- We all have different Stimulation and Excitement quotas. Recognize what your quota is and discover how you are currently filling it. Face up to mixed feelings in yourself and others.
- No one seeks negative stimulation deliberately, but when they don't know how to get positive stimulation, they turn to negative sources.
- Understand the plus side and minus side of defiant behavior—in yourself and those around you.
- Learn to fill your Stimulation and Excitement Quota creatively for more high quality time in your life.

# 5

## THE GUILT TRAP—WORLD CHAMPION TIME WASTER

Guilt is implicated in more wasted time and poor time arrangement than any other single emotion. That is why understanding the relationship between guilt and time is vital.

### DON'T CLOUD YOUR THINKING WITH GUILT

The person voicing the following indictment of guilt speaks for many of us:

"When I finally sit down to concentrate on something important, I'm plagued with guilty feelings about dozens of other things—the mess around me, the letters I haven't written, the calls I must make, the people I should see, minor chores I haven't done. So I get up and attend to something that I feel guilty about. Then I'm out of the mood to concentrate. I never have enough time to do what's really important."

This comment pinpoints a major danger of guilt. When we feel guilty, we don't do our best thinking. We often end up in a flurry of activity on matters that are not of primary importance. We may even feel the suffocating grip of paralyzing inaction. Despite a massive attack of painful guilt, we don't do anything but procrastinate. We put off doing what is really important—sometimes until it is too late.

When we succumb to guilt feelings, we set up a barrier to effective time management. You can overcome this barrier more easily when you understand the origins of guilt and why it is often inappropriate.

### HOW TO SPOT PHONY GUILT

Guilt can be real and appropriate. If someone commits murder, batters a child, or steals another's life savings, these are valid reasons to feel guilty. On the whole, however, the guilt we let rob us of our time isn't real guilt—it's phony because it's inappropriate.

Symptoms of inappropriate guilt spring from many different causes. Some of us feel guilty if we don't do everything perfectly, or don't keep busy every moment. Others feel guilty about enjoying themselves, or about feeling good when someone else is unhappy. Some people may even feel guilty about feeling guilty.

Most of the time-wasting guilt feelings that we allow to intrude on our time are related to the less important situations or chores—a messy back closet, an overflowing garage, a dinner invitation, the need to catch up on current events.

Conditions like these don't merit the depth of guilt many of us feel. That kind of guilt is unhealthy, unproductive, and inappropriate.

Before we go further, here is my definition of guilt: *A feeling of deviation from a relevant standard.* I use the word "relevant" because we feel guilty only when we have not fulfilled a standard for which we believe we are responsible.

Examine your own guilt feelings carefully. You may find that they are generated by a failure to meet an outdated standard. At one time that standard may have been meaningful, but it is now inappropriate.

## PURITANS AND PIONEERS

Whatever your ethnic heritage, it's hard to escape the influence of the Puritan work ethic. It still characterizes much in our society, even though it doesn't fit today's reality.

In 1650, the motto "Idle hands are the Devil's workshop" had validity for the early New England pioneers. There was a continent to conquer, a hostile environment to tame. They *had* to work constantly, and there was very little time to do anything else. So they elevated hard work to the level of moral superiority. It helped keep their noses to the grindstone. "Keep busy" really meant "Work hard if you want to survive."

Over the years, conditions changed, but the concept of hard work for its own sake became ingrained in the American way of life. This attitude is still prevalent, although it is no longer realistic.

Today, technological advances have produced a wealth of labor-saving devices. We have more freedom and a greater range of choices and activities than ever before in history.

We have the opportunity to balance work and play, to create richly rewarding lives. We do not have to be engaged in productive work all the time, but the belief that we *should* be persists. Many of us feel we cannot escape guilt feelings even when we know we deserve time to sit back, relax, and do nothing.

## THE TREADMILL OF BUSYNESS— AN OUTDATED STANDARD

After a recent speech I made to a professional association, an old acquaintance came up and asked, "Are you busy these days?" In the preceding months, I'd managed to achieve a rewarding balance between work and recreation. It was with a real sense of accomplishment that I replied, "No, I'm not busy all the time." Much to my chagrin, my acquaintance looked embarrassed. He backed away, muttering, "I'm sure things will get better—you'll be busy again soon." Before I could explain, he beat a hasty retreat.

His remark reflected the old cultural standard that glorifies busyness. He didn't consider whether my energies were well directed or productive, nor what I was *accomplishing* with my time.

Comments like this can also have deeper meanings. For example, consider the statement, "I'm so busy I never have a minute to myself." How often have you heard variations on that theme? Such comments may really mean, "I'm busy, therefore I'm needed. I'm worthwhile." Busyness becomes the standard people use to measure their worth as human beings. They believe it's the only way to justify their right to existence.

Personal worth does not depend upon what you do. You have value as a human being regardless of your activities. The prestige or economic value of your work has no bearing on your worth or your right to human dignity. If these two issues are confused, it's common to fall into the trap of feeling guilty about what you do or don't do with your time. The real issue is to understand that *you deserve to be here*. You have the right to live your life as fully as you desire.

## THE PERFECTION SYNDROME

Preoccupation with hard work and busyness isn't the only standard that can produce inappropriate guilt. Many of us further burden ourselves by the perfection syndrome. People in this snare feel they must do everything perfectly. They strive to maintain the cleanest house in town, the neatest desk in their department. Their lives are so completely organized that *every* task must be finished, and finished perfectly.

The media bombards us with images that contribute to these inappropriate standards of perfection. Television and magazine ads show us floors that always gleam, people who never slouch or get fat, children whose clothes are always clean and wrinkle-free.

If you make such standards a part of your life, you are setting yourself up to carry a heavy load of guilt. You lose the ability to make thoughtful judgments about your work. You are likely to waste enormous amounts of time on tasks that don't really matter.

## "I SHOULD BE DOING BETTER"

This concept is an offshoot of the perfection syndrome. The problem is that most people who use this phrase don't even define what "better" means. *They fall short of the standard without ever knowing what the standard is.*

I once worked with a dedicated senior executive who continually plagued himself with feelings of guilt about not "doing better." No matter how much he accomplished, he never felt it was enough. He'd become a chronic workaholic. His family hardly knew what he looked like. He wanted to change, but didn't know how to free himself from that guilt. I pointed out that he was denying himself a courtesy he would extend to any of his staff. He had never clearly defined exactly what "better" meant in his situation.

He sat down and analyzed his job responsibilities. He defined exactly what and how much he was responsible for. He set specific standards for measuring his performance so he would know if and when he missed the mark.

He didn't change overnight. He's been following his new regime for several months now, but he still feels an occasional twinge of guilt when he walks out of his office at 5:30 P.M. and sees members of his staff still working on *their* projects. But he keeps right on walking. He reminds himself, "I concentrate on doing what is most important; I don't let guilt feelings run my life." He can deal with the guilt feelings now; it gets easier every day. And he knows he's not wasting any of his time on inappropriate guilt.

## PORTABLE GUILT

Guilt arising from standards that are unrealistic, irrelevant, and ill-defined is a slippery enemy. If you clean up the messy closet you feel guilty about, you will find that you now feel guilty about that pile of magazines you haven't read yet. One thing leads to another. Don't believe that you can ever satisfy free-floating, unrealistic guilt by "doing better," "doing everything perfectly," or "doing enough." There will always be something else you can feel guilty about.

## SPRINGING THE GUILT TRAP

Even if you feel guilty, go ahead and do what you know is most important. *Continuing, constructive action toward what really counts remedies inappropriate guilt.* Ask yourself these questions when you are feeling guilty:

1. Specifically, what am I feeling guilty about?
2. Is this something that is really an essential or central concern to me or someone else?
3. Today, how can I best *do* what really counts?

The answers to these questions will help you grasp the keys to successful time management: identifying the central concerns in your life; understanding the motivations involved; and doing what really counts every day. These are the major themes of this book, and they will be developed in detail in later chapters. The techniques you will learn will help you do what is most important without letting guilt feelings run your life.

## A TRUE STORY

If you wait until you have done all the little things you feel guilty about, you may never get to the heart of what you really want. A painful situation that I wish had not been true brought this lesson home to me.

"This afternoon they told Margaret she has only one more week to live." The words I was hearing over the telephone stunned me. David was telling me that Margaret, his wife and my special friend, was dying. The doctors had finally diagnosed the source of her sudden streak of splitting headaches as "increased intracranial pressure secondary to a brain tumor."

It sounded unreal; I couldn't believe it. Margaret was only forty-two. I'd seen her just four weeks earlier. She had been as blithe and full of vitality as ever. She and her husband had an exceptionally happy marriage, two wonderful sons, rewarding careers—everything to live for. I couldn't believe that she would die so suddenly, in such a cruelly unexpected way.

Margaret did not get a miracle reprieve. She did die. But two days before her death, we talked on the telephone. Even though pain-killing drugs slowed her familiar voice to halting phrases, her words rang with unquenchable spirit and profound wisdom. The memory of that conversation has made a difference in my life ever since.

"For some reason, during these last six months, I've been thinking more about how I spend my time," Margaret said. "I'd always thought of myself as primarily career-oriented, but I now realize that my family is most important to me. I've been concentrating on spending more time with them."

As I gripped the phone, struggling to control my tears, Margaret went on to say something that was deeply significant to me.

"It's so much easier to face what I am facing now because I've spent my time doing what really counts."

Long after the call ended, I sat thinking about Margaret. I remembered visiting her at home one day. Her desk in the corner of the family study was overflowing with papers. She laughed as she gestured toward it and said, "I guess I should feel guilty about how messy that looks, but there are so many things more important to me than having a clean desk. The things that count come first."

I had an even more poignant memory of Margaret, one that illustrates how her concentration on what was most important to her brought beauty to others.

Some months before, Margaret had told me about a project she and her husband were involved in with their young sons. They were making rubbings of late nineteenth-century manhole covers. Every Saturday they would board the subway, armed with rice paper, tape, brushes, and charcoal. They'd head for one of the older neighborhoods in the city where there were some wonderful old manhole covers. When they discovered one they liked, they'd get right down to work. One of the boys would brush away the dirt, the other would tape the rice paper. Inevitably, their activity would attract a crowd of children, curious to know what two adults and two boys were doing crouched over a manhole.

I remembered Margaret smiling as she related how fascinated the neighborhood children would become. She knew it helped them see their neighborhood in a different way. She loved the idea that as a result of her family's activity, these children became more alive to the beauty of ordinary, everyday things in the world around them.

As I sat by the phone, reliving my memories of Margaret, I thought over what she had said to me about doing what counts. I realized that if I were in a similar situation, I couldn't make that statement. I wasn't spending my time on the things that really mattered. I was allowing too much of it to slip away while I attended to things I felt guilty about. Were it not for Margaret's words, I might never have taken the time to discover what really counts in my own life and to do it every day.

Learning how to identify what counts most for you in your life is the thrust of Chapter 11. You will discover how to determine what you most want to accomplish and what quality of lifestyle you want.

Few of us must face a crisis like Margaret's, but we all have just so much time to invest. Don't rob yourself of even a minute of your share by feeling guilty.

### DO WHAT REALLY COUNTS FIRST— AND DO IT FIRST

You don't have to accept every opportunity for guilt. Understand the source of your guilt feelings by asking yourself these questions:

1. What is the standard I'm feeling responsible for?
2. Is it relevant for me now?
3. Are my guilt feelings appropriate?
4. How does this feeling of guilt relate to what really counts?

*Every day* continue your program to identify what counts most. *Do it first*, even if it means putting off secondary matters, doing them less perfectly, getting someone else to do them, or not doing them at all. Don't allow yourself to get mired down by irrelevant and inappropriate feelings of guilt.

## THIS DAY IS YOURS

Accept the full gift of this moment—you deserve it. Take hold of today. Use it, enjoy it in the most exciting, creative way you can. This is a day for you to do the things that are most important to you. This is a day to know how good it is to be alive.

You are a part of the universe. You have a right to be here. You have a right to all the happiness and all the good things you can possibly receive. This is your time—you deserve to live it fully.

# 6

# WHAT YOU LEARNED ABOUT TIME FROM MOM AND DAD

As a child, you received many messages about time from your parents. They may have been positive or negative, clear or mixed, spoken or nonverbal. These messages may even vary for different children in the same family. The ideas we absorb are always highly individual. What they have in common is impact—your perception of your parents' time use is a strong influence on your time use today.

Many people are unaware that this early childhood programming forms the basis for their current time management style. Day after day, they repeat patterns learned long ago. This chapter will help you discover what early messages you learned, and how they influence your time use now.

## SORTING OUT THE MESSAGES

Sometimes, the productive messages that parents communicate are verbal. Betty V., financial executive in a large chemical corporation, told me that one of her mother's favorite sayings contributed to her success. She grew up hearing the gentle but firm reminder, "Duty first." As a child, she learned to finish her work before she went out to play. Today that old message, "Duty first," helps her organize her priorities. She's earned a well-deserved reputation for consistently getting the right things done on time.

Another successful woman in the same company never actually heard anyone say, "Duty first," but she got the message anyway. Her mother was a legal secretary who worked five days a week, and had an hour's daily commute. Grocery shopping was done on Saturdays, and her mother insisted that chores came before outings or excursions. The children learned that if they wanted to speed up departure time for a movie or the beach, they had to help with the shopping first.

Jim C., real estate broker, consulted me about a time problem that had been plaguing him all his life. He wasted enormous amounts of time struggling to get himself going on the job each day. When he recalled how his parents used time, he got in touch with the cause of his problem. His father procrastinated from Sunday through Saturday. He was forever putting things off. When minor repairs around the house needed attention, his father took months to get around to them. The summer window screens would still be up in November. The storm windows weren't taken down until July. The Christmas tree was still standing in February. As a child, the broker got the message, "You can always do it tomorrow." Unconsciously, he was complicating his time by following that unproductive message.

## SAME MESSAGE—DIFFERENT ROUTE

Many people receive the same messages in different ways. One child may hear, "Keep busy! Idle hands are the Devil's workshop!" and develop a preoccupation with busyness in later life. This message might produce fear or distrust of unstructured leisure. It may even interfere with wholehearted enjoyment of good times.

Another child may never have heard that Puritan motto, but will pick up the same message. Perhaps he observed his parents in a never-ending stream of busy activities—his mother knitting wherever she went; his father invariably bringing home a briefcase stuffed with office work. As an adult, this child may develop similar habits. He may believe that he, too, must always keep busy.

## MIXED MESSAGES

Although some messages are clear, others can be mixed. Parents may say one thing, but do another, like that old proverb "Do as I say, not as I do." The child is not always able to make the distinction.

Philip is an executive in an advertising firm. His world is filled with deadlines, but for years he constantly missed them. His trouble stemmed from the "Just One More Thing" syndrome.

When Philip learned to understand childhood messages, he discovered the root of his problem. He explained that both his parents were forever harping on the importance of being on time. Their actions, however, communicated quite another message.

If the family was setting out for an appointment or an excursion, the same thing always happened. The parents would nag the children to hurry up, get ready, get in the car. Philip and his two brothers would pile into the car, all set to go. Invariably, they'd have to wait for their parents. Dad would take time to wind up the garden hose. Mom would make one last tour through the house, checking that all the doors were locked. They were rarely on time anywhere. What they did, rather than what they said, formed the message for Philip.

## DELIBERATE OR NOT, IT STILL MAKES A DIFFERENCE

As you learned in the previous chapter, we don't deliberately seek negative stimulation and excitement. Sometimes, such behavior stems from watching our parents seek negative stimulation. Remember the father of five with the stationwagon full of children? As they rounded every curve in the highway, nervously scouting the horizon for a service station, those children were getting a strong message. Their father was showing them a negative way to get stimulation and excitement.

Some children resort to negative stimulation because positive sources aren't readily available. A child who receives little or no attention or praise from his parents for constructive behavior soon discovers the rewards of negative behavior. A series of "accidents" may occur. A fishbowl gets knocked over. Scissors are dropped down the toilet. A peanut butter and jelly sandwich gets mashed into the rug. The child gets attention and life is suddenly more exciting. The seeds of negative stimulation have been sown.

## WHAT MESSAGES DID YOU LEARN?

Here are some of the most common areas of psychological programming relating to time. What messages did you pick up about these subjects when you were a child?

Being on time _____

Being late _____

Not finishing on time _____

Duty first _____

Negative attention _____

Promptness _____

Being early _____

Knowing when to leave _____

Arriving ahead of time _____

Being the first one there _____

Being the last to leave _____

Being the first to leave _____

Dawdling _____

Clocks _____

Are there any other messages about time that come to mind?

· _____

_____

_____

_____

What impact do they have on your time management style today?

_____

_____

_____

Take a few minutes to consider what you learned about time while you were growing up. Discover which messages are still helpful and identify those that no longer serve you well. This will help speed up the process of designing the time management program that will work best for you *today*.

## REINFORCE THE BEST

- Identify the messages you learned about time while you were growing up.
- *Remember that although childhood is a strong influence, you need not let it totally control adult behavior.* You can change your behavior today if you choose to do so.
- Most habits—productive or nonproductive—stem from repetition and reinforcement. That's why they can be changed.
- Build on early programming that works for you.

# 7

# DOING IT YOUR WAY—
## ADD STYLE TO TIME
## MANAGEMENT

---

**S**mooth and successful time management depends on personal style—how you manage your time, not just what you
accomplish. Because you learned a certain style of time management when you were a child, that doesn't mean you cannot change if you want to. Because one person uses a time
technique in a certain way, that doesn't mean you must use
the technique in the same way. You may come across as rigid
or phony if you do, because it doesn't suit your personality.
There's no fixed formula for style.

### MORE ART THAN SCIENCE—
### THE FIVE CLASSIC ELEMENTS OF DESIGN

The elements of a personal time management style that is responsive to your current needs relate more closely to art than
science. Specifically, these are the five elements of artistic
design that were first articulated by the ancient Greeks thousands of years ago. They are as useful today as they were
then.

The five elements of design are: order, balance, contrast,
unity, and harmony. Each one is important. Together they
form a whole that far exceeds the sum of its parts.

*Order* is what people often seek when they say, "I've got to
get organized." It answers the universal human longing for a
discernible pattern of life. It involves knowledge of the connection between the past, the present, and the future. It gives
life a sense of direction and movement. That is why doing
something each day toward fulfilling your long-term objectives is so satisfying. It provides this needed sense of direction.

*Balance* offers a sense of stability. You can achieve it by
planning your time to include:

• recurring activities at regularly scheduled times

47

&bull; continuity in your contacts with key people in your life.

*Contrast* adds spark and stimulation. It's the basis for the old saying, "Variety is the spice of life." Periods of high productivity are more satisfying when they are mixed with rest and recreation. You can enjoy contrast by having both:

&bull; creative and routine work
&bull; mental and physical activities
&bull; time alone and time with others
&bull; structured and unstructured time.

*Unity* conveys a sense of belonging and collectiveness. You experience a greater feeling of unity when you know that your actions contribute to an embracing whole. Another way to add unity is to ask yourself, "How can I enable this activity to contribute to what I most want?" The finishing fully technique (see page 103) heightens a pleasing sense of unity.

*Harmony* relates to the similarities in the ways you invest your time. It means recognizing these similarities, and discovering connections and relationships. It fosters a smooth-flowing, well-coordinated, responsive whole. You can achieve harmony by:

&bull; spotting persistent problems, trends, and patterns
&bull; grouping related activities
&bull; doing all central concerns and top priorities first.

## THE RIGHT RECIPE FOR EACH OCCASION

The development of an attractive time management style depends on the right blending of time techniques for the given situation or moment. Even if one idea is good in itself, like any of the five design elements, don't use it exclusively. Make sure you use the technique that is best *at this moment.*

Sally S. is a top-notch executive assistant who prides herself on her time management skills. One day she was on the phone giving information to a freelance artist. Midway through the conversation, Sally noticed that her boss was urgently signalling Sally to enter her office. Sally ignored the handwaving and her boss's increasingly exasperated expression. She was concentrating on doing one thing at a time, and she wanted to finish fully before beginning something else. Since she needed only five minutes to complete her call, she reasoned that she should finish it before responding to her boss.

Finally Sally hung up and appeared at her boss's door. She was greeted with an angry blast. Her boss had had three people on a conference call, and needed a document that she couldn't find. When Sally did not respond to her signal, her boss had to tell the others she'd call them back.

Sally was an ace organizer who could have found that document in seconds. If she had told the artist she'd call back and responded to her boss, there would have been only a few minutes' lapse in her own conversation. As it was, it took half an hour to hook up the four-person conference call again.

Sally's style was rigid rather than responsive. She was concentrating on doing one thing at a time. Although a good idea in itself, it wasn't the right procedure in that instance.

Good style means blending the right combination of techniques that are best at that moment. Stay flexible. It will help in many areas of your life besides time management. It is reassuring to know that whatever your circumstances were at one time, you can always reconsider the situation. You can take the action that is best for you right now. *You always have a number of alternatives from which to choose. There are many paths to take toward your desired destination.* This is not only a major idea behind good time management, it's a major element in good mental health.

## NO COOKBOOK SOLUTION

There's no universal formula for achieving the beauty of all five design elements in your time management style. That's a matter of personal exploration and experimentation. You may never be able to explain how you achieved the combination that is best for you. Once you've developed the art of doing so, however, you'll know it. It will feel graceful and right because:

- you have selected the techniques that work best for you
- you know how to tailor them to fit your personality *and* your situation.

## PUT IT TOGETHER WITH STYLE

The following chapters tell you how to discover more about your personal time management style. The rest of the book offers techniques that you can select to suit your personality, problems, and situation. It provides the tools you'll need to design and develop the style that fits you best.

For now, the important things to remember are:

- Developing the time management style that's best for you is more art than science.
- Although there is no one answer, there are specific techniques you can use to develop the style that suits you best.
- Successful style involves five classic elements of design: order, balance, contrast, unity, and harmony. Each is important; together they add up to an attractive style.
- Stay flexible. There are many paths to take toward your desired destination—you always have a number of alternatives.

# 8

## COMPULSIVE TIME/ CHOICE TIME— PROBLEM AND POTENTIAL

---

Have you ever wondered why one person will hear about a new time technique and immediately put it into action, while an equally bright person in a similar situation doesn't? The second person may think it's a good idea—may even start to use it a few times. Ultimately, however, he or she will let it drop, never reaping the benefits. Why? The answer usually lies in the difference between choice time and compulsive time.

### DEALING FROM BLIND SPOTS

People who don't put relevant time techniques to work for themselves are usually operating from a blind spot. They know what to do, but they don't do it. They keep making the same mistakes with their time. They have let themselves fall into the habit of *compulsive time use.*

For example, two specialists in the same company were exposed to a classic time technique—handle papers only once. Both men said it would help reduce their workload, but each had a different response.

One of the men put it to work immediately, and revolutionized his paperwork. "For the first time in my career, my desk top looks civilized—not like a paper jungle. The technique makes such common sense, I don't know why I didn't think of it myself."

However, the other specialist still wrestled with a flood of paperwork. "I thought that technique was a darn good idea when I first heard it. I still do. But here I am—still drowning in paper. I go through my 'in' basket a dozen times a day, pick something up, and look at it. Then I wonder if I have enough information to make a decision. I don't want to make a mistake, so I put it down again. I know shuffling papers doesn't accomplish anything. I know I should handle each paper only once. But I just can't get myself to do it."

This dynamic crops up hundreds of times in my management seminars. It explains why so many intelligent people fail to put time techniques to work for themselves. What's "just common sense" to one person remains out of reach for someone else.

Perhaps it is the technique of finishing fully (see page 103). A man knows he needs to write a letter. He finally writes it, but he doesn't finish the job. He delays addressing the envelope. He doesn't paste on a stamp. It takes him three days to drop it in the mailbox. He doesn't finish fully although he knows the value of the idea. Again, there's a blind spot.

Consider yourself. What are some of the time techniques you know but rarely use?

Compulsive time use is part of the human condition. It merely means that many of us feel compelled to function in a habitual way even when it is not helpful. At these times, *how* we act overshadows the *purpose* of our actions.

All of us get caught up in this kind of behavior at some time or another. For instance, when I'm feeling especially pressured, I start to hurry. When I hurry I move around more, but I don't necessarily accomplish more. I find myself standing at my desk hurriedly half-doing five things at the same time. Then I recognize that I'm functioning from one of my blind spots, in an unproductive, compulsive mode. I take a few seconds to slow down and breathe deeply, then I sit down and think more clearly.

Examine your own time management style in this light, and you will discover some important and revealing patterns. You will understand your areas of compulsive time use. It's important to know what they are.

## CHOOSING THE BEST TECHNIQUES

*You don't need to learn all the time techniques in this book. You only need to concentrate on the few that will help you deal with your blind spots—your compulsive time uses.* All the other techniques will seem familiar to you. You will embrace them like old friends. You can put them to work almost without thought.

## "WHAT'S WRONG WITH COMPULSIVE TIME?"

Compulsive time use is not necessarily negative, it's just less than the best. You don't do your clearest thinking when you are operating from compulsion. You block yourself from getting the optimum return on your time investment. You can accomplish what you want through compulsive time use, but you pay a higher price. You achieve *better results* when you learn to transfer your energies to choice time. What's more, you will achieve those greater results faster, more easily, with increased satisfaction.

One Hour's Time Investment  =  Desired Results

Compulsive Time  =

Choice Time  =

## DIFFERENCES BETWEEN COMPULSION AND CHOICE

| *Compulsive Time* | *Choice Time* |
|---|---|
| Low Productivity & Efficiency | High Productivity & Effectiveness |
| Stereotyped Solutions | Creative Solutions |
| Rigid Responses | Flexible Responses |
| Habitual Reactions to Situations and Needs | Reactions to Actual Situations and Real Needs |
| Emphasis on *How* Things Are Done | Emphasis on *What* Things Are Done |

Diagnosing your own compulsive time use is the first step toward gaining more *choice time*. It frees you to choose techniques that will reduce your compulsive time use. You'll know which techniques can work for you *and* the importance of motivating yourself to use them frequently.

## THE POTENTIAL OF CHOICE TIME

When you operate from choice, you consistently do your best thinking. You are free to explore the full range of alternatives open to you. You can concentrate totally on what you are doing. You can delve deeper into problems and uncover real causes.

Choice time offers a special bonus in personal relationships. You can understand others more fully because you are not as preoccupied with *how* things are done. You will be giving people your full attention. You will be able to enrich your time with your friends and family in dozens of rewarding ways.

## SHAKING LOOSE FROM SUPERFICIALS

When we function from the blind spot of compulsive time use, we trap ourselves on the surface of problems. We don't get in touch with the deeper implications of the situation. When we operate from choice, we can get below the superficial symptoms and discover the real issues and root problems. We can achieve better results.

The head of a construction company explained how an understanding of these issues improved his time use and his ability to make better decisions. "I used to rush around like crazy, always jumping from one problem to the next. I came up with some good solutions, but they weren't always the best. The long-range problems were never solved. I was too busy putting out brushfires to identify their causes.

"After I'd been exposed to the compulsion/choice concept, I realized how I'd been limiting myself. I decided to take some time away from the day-to-day rush. I started coming in an hour early and going swimming during lunch. I used the time to think about the larger issues—how to improve the company's overall profitability. One day, as I was swimming, I realized that we could get a much better return on our assets if we divested one of our problem operations and invested the capital in real estate holdings. In the past I had frequently solved the wrong problems. By freeing myself to operate from choice, I've made an amazing improvement in my time use."

The vice president of a growing distribution company learned about the concept of choice time from his secretary.

New contract negotiations made it necessary to produce employee information handbooks for the company's five warehouses scattered across the country. Since the details of pay scales and benefits were different for all five, the executive prepared for the tedious, time-consuming task of producing five separate handbooks.

However, his secretary took time to probe beneath the immediate surface of the problem. She pointed out that they could draft a basic format, and leave blanks for the different details. The five plant managers could fill in the specific details that applied to their employees.

This solution saved both time and money, and gave the vice president a new handle on the value of choice time. His company is still growing fast, but he's solving the right problems.

Choice time can be applied to small problems just as successfully. For example, Henry M. loved indoor greenery and had a house full of plants. But the row of large Boston ferns in the living room was a problem—they shed their leaves constantly and Henry and his roommate were forever cleaning up.

One day Henry took the time to think the problem through. His nurseryman pointed out that the light and humidity in the living room were wrong for Boston ferns. Henry traded them in for less temperamental Grape Ivy. The ivy thrived. He solved the problem rather than merely working on the symptoms.

## SOLVE THE RIGHT PROBLEMS

When you operate from choice time, you solve the *right* problems. You don't waste your time solving just *any* problems. The benefits are both organizational and personal. That's why it's worthwhile learning the techniques that will help reduce your compulsive time use. You will expand your choice time. You will get the best return on your time investments consistently.

Now let's take a look at the five types of compulsive time use—Hurry Up, Be Perfect, Please Me, Try Hard, and Be Strong. Surprisingly, these five types cover the entire spectrum of compulsive time use.

# 9

## THE FIVE TYPES OF COMPULSIVE TIME

The psychological theory of the five major types of compulsive behavior was developed for therapeutic application by Taibi Kahler, a brilliant psychologist from Little Rock, Arkansas. He chose the following highly descriptive titles for each type: Hurry Up, Be Perfect, Please Me, Try Hard, and Be Strong.

When I first encountered Dr. Kahler's theory, it seemed too simplistic, although I knew that he had achieved remarkable therapeutic results. I objected to the idea that there were "only" five roles. Surely my experience would reveal several others.

In the years that followed, I became convinced that Dr. Kahler was correct. His theory clearly illustrates how a great deal of sophisticated psychological material can be condensed into nontechnical language. Furthermore, I discovered that his theory applied to time management as well.

This chapter describes the five types in detail. Some will seem more familiar to you than others. Although we engage in all of them some of the time, most of us specialize in two roles. Spot the two that fit your use of time most closely. They aren't the same for everybody.

Remember, you don't have to learn hundreds of time techniques, only those that relate to your most frequent compulsive time uses. Techniques that relate to choice time will seem just like common sense. You may be using them already without realizing it. In any event, you'll be able to put those techniques to work almost instantly.

After each description, I have listed some of the techniques that are most helpful in reducing that type of compulsive behavior. Detailed explanations of these techniques will follow in later chapters. Use these brief lists as a handy guide for selecting the techniques you want to learn.

## HURRY UP

People playing a Hurry Up role *always* rush, whether it's necessary or not. They rush to meet deadlines. If they have two days to accomplish something, they'll find a way to delay until the last minute, because they get a lot of excitement from rushing. It isn't always the best way to get the stimulation they need, and it isn't usually a necessary or efficient investment of time.

A highly successful salesman who plays a Hurry Up role built his original ten small accounts into a total of thirty. Fifteen generate 90 percent of his income. But he runs himself ragged trying to service all thirty accounts. He doesn't stop to realize that this isn't the best way to invest his time and energy. He could turn over the original ten accounts to a less experienced person on the sales staff. This would free him to spend more time on the accounts that really pay off. And he'd have the time to get even more large accounts. The ten small accounts would still get the service they require, and the organization would benefit, too. Some other salesperson would be getting experience that would pay off for the company as a whole.

Some techniques for the Hurry Up role:

- Do central concerns first. (See Chapter 12.)
- Give yourself daily think-time for planning and evaluation. (See Chapters 10 and 15.)
- First clarify what you want to accomplish before deciding how to do it. (See Chapter 11.)
- Study your personal calendar whenever you have a spare moment of "time in." (See Chapter 15.)
- Satisfy your personal Stimulation and Excitement Quota positively; plan your time with this need in mind. (See Chapters 3 and 17.)
- Set mini deadlines rather than one big final deadline. (See Chapter 14.)

## BE PERFECT

People who play a Be Perfect role waste valuable time on trivia or marginal matters because they feel they must perform *every* task perfectly. A competent graduate student recopies all notes or memos if a word is crossed out. She straightens her desk top five and six times a day. She works beyond the point of diminishing return on everything she does. She told me that she vividly recalled her father's response whenever she brought home a school paper marked "96%" or even "98%." Invariably, he'd say, "Why not 100%?"

Be Perfects also have difficulty admitting a mistake, and they waste time defending it or trying to cover it up. They document explanations for the mistake, rather than admitting and correcting the error.

Their ability to make decisions suffers as well. Every decision must be perfect, even on an inconsequential matter. One group of Be Perfects worked on a committee to prepare a project report. They spent ninety minutes one day deciding whether to label the report's supplemental material "Attachment" or "Tab." They were intelligent, competent, analytical people, but they were playing the Be Perfect role. They felt compelled to find the *perfect* term for those supplemental papers.

In their personal lives, people assuming a Be Perfect role seek out perfect relationships. They spend considerable time searching for the ideal man or the ideal woman. At the first sign of clay feet on their latest idol, they leave, compelled to find someone else. Since ideal men and women are rare, their search is never-ending.

Stacks of newspapers and magazines often surround the perfectionist. If you feel that you have to read *everything,* it's easy to generate a backlog of reading.

Accountants and lawyers often play Be Perfect roles. If you just want a rough financial estimate, a Be Perfect accountant will provide a detailed report that took five hours to prepare. You will receive much more information than you need to reach your decision. If you ask a Be Perfect lawyer for some general business advice, you will wind up with an exhaustive, heavily annotated summary of the Uniform Commercial Code.

People playing Be Perfect roles often postpone completion of a project because of their compulsion to do everything perfectly. Scientists and engineers often exhibit this behavior. They may work on a project for six months and compile enough data to produce 90 percent of their findings. But they'll feel compelled to spend another eighteen months perfecting that last 10 percent. No matter what it costs, or how appropriate it is, they drive themselves to produce perfect findings. Others may postpone a project entirely because they know they can't do it perfectly.

Some time techniques for the Be Perfect role:

- Avoid perfectionism on things that are secondary or marginal and stick to your estimate. (See Chapter 12.)
- Handle papers only once, or at least take some action each time you pick them up. (See Chapter 25.)
- Use headlines in books and magazines as signposts for material to read in detail. Don't feel compelled to read everything word for word. (See Chapter 25.)
- If you waste time searching for something, substitute something else whenever possible.
- Estimate how much time projects are really worth to you and stick to your estimate. (See Chapter 12.)
- Every day, deliberately do at least one thing imperfectly.

## PLEASE ME

Do you often say "Yes" when you want to say "No"? You're probably playing a Please Me role. Please Me types often have the best intentions in the world. They don't want to hurt someone's feelings. They hate to give bad news. They want to avoid damaging anyone's morale. Therefore, Please Me types frequently overcommit themselves. They say "Yes" to so many people that they aren't able to deliver all they promise. They wind up disappointing others and hurting themselves.

Gene L. was working on a government grant and had a Please Me as project director. This Please Me knew for months that the grant would not be renewed, but avoided telling his staff. He didn't want them to worry and hated giving bad news to anyone. As a result, no one on the staff was prepared for the funding cut-off date. None of them had taken time to update their resumes or think about finding another job.

Gene wouldn't have been happy to know the grant wasn't renewed, but he would have appreciated the information earlier. He would have had the time to develop contacts for his next job.

When I first came to work in San Francisco, I let myself fall into the Please Me trap. I was right out of college and suddenly conscious of my student appearance. I wanted a more professional image for job hunting, so I went to buy a coat that would improve my look. I tried on several. Then I let myself get talked into buying a mustard brown coat with a high collar. It was a terrible color for me. At the time, I wore tortoise-shell glasses, no makeup, and had mousy brown hair; the effect was totally unbecoming. But I didn't want to hurt the saleswoman's feelings, so I bought it. I didn't recognize the Please Me role then, but whenever I find myself falling into this type of behavior today, one mental flash of that coat propels me onto a different track.

Some techniques for the Please Me role:

- Practice how to say "No" in advance. (See Chapter 31.)
- Tell others directly what your objectives are and what *you* want. (See Chapter 31.)
- Give yourself sorting-out time each day to think through your priorities and plan activities. (See Chapters 10 and 12.)
- Every day, do something toward what *you* most want to accomplish in your lifetime and that fits your long-term lifestyle. (See Chapter 11.)
- Use a written action sheet or a "to do" list during daily "time in." (See Chapter 15.)

### TRY HARD

People who play Try Hard roles do a lot of sighing. They thrive on suffering and talk constantly about how hard they work. Often, they have two vertical lines etched deeply between their eyebrows. Look into their early childhood programming; you'll usually find a parent who constantly reminded, "Well, at least you tried. That's what counts."

Try Hards don't look at the *results* of their time investment. They concentrate on getting "A for effort" instead. They are often found in organizations that don't have clearly defined objectives. They get credit for trying hard, and they don't have to account for their failure to achieve the best results in the least amount of time. Good old Charlie may feel he deserves a lot of credit for burning the midnight oil on those progress reports. But if you need results, you'd probably be a lot happier if he spent less time talking about the effort he's putting in. He might get the job done faster.

Finding simpler ways to accomplish your objectives does not detract from the quality of the result. Try Hards don't grasp this idea. They believe that effort is what counts. They don't focus on results.

Trying hard is only a process, not an end in itself. You limit yourself by concentrating on effort rather than on results. First focus clearly on the results you want. You will free yourself to accomplish more in less time, without unnecessary effort. Work hard, but work on the right things.

Some techniques for the Try Hard role:

- Clarify objectives before deciding upon activities. (See Chapter 11.)
- Give the right kind of time to the right activities; carve out blocks of time for major jobs. (See Chapter 12.)
- Divide big projects into smaller, more workable units. (See Chapter 14.)
- Use gadgets such as recorders and calculators to multiply your time. (See Chapter 25.)
- Ask yourself every day, "What is an easier way to accomplish this?"

## BE STRONG

Traditional time management techniques often work for the Be Strong type. These methods emphasize discipline and unemotional evaluation. That's meat and drink for the Be Strongs. They feel the only key to better time management is "more self-discipline."

They don't believe in relying on anyone for help. They think it's just a question of adherence to stricter schedules. Be Strongs accomplish a lot, but they pay a price. They waste a lot of their time (and that of others) because they won't ask for help when it's appropriate to do so. They avoid any situation where they might appear weak.

Here's a typical demonstration of Be Strong behavior. A driver is looking for the right turnoff on the highway in an unfamiliar area. There's no map of the locality in the car, but he or she would never stop to ask for directions. Whether it's a salesman on the way to an important meeting or a Den Mother driving a stationwagon full of Cub Scouts, a Be Strong feels compelled to keep going no matter what—even if it wastes valuable time. Be Strongs rarely ask for help.

Many women who achieve success on the executive level have Be Strong programming. In the early stages of their careers, they felt they had to demonstrate that they could handle the job without any assistance. They trained themselves not to express feelings of need or frustration that might be judged as "feminine weakness." As a result, many never learned how to delegate or use staff support effectively.

Line managers who play the Be Strong role can waste enormous amounts of time. They often distrust other departments and want everything in their own tight control. They will duplicate information from the accounting department by keeping "cuff records." They demand their own copying equipment so they don't have to rely on central services. They want their own computer. They feel compelled to entrench themselves. They want to create a situation that ensures they don't have to ask anyone for help.

Some techniques for the Be Strong role:

- Build in reinforcements and rewards. (See Chapter 17.)
- Give yourself both "time in" for productive action and "time out" for rest and relaxation.
- Set realistic deadlines for yourself and others. (See Chapter 13.)
- If you find yourself procrastinating, discover the feelings you are avoiding. (See Chapter 16.)

## ABOUT ALL FIVE ROLES

Some people respond to these concepts by saying, "I don't do any of those things!" Great; if that's accurate, you are operating from choice all the time. But that's not the case for most of us. Typically, we spend from 50–90 percent of our time in compulsive roles. Even if you are the exception, it's helpful to understand how the rest of us operate.

If you feel you need more information before you can make a decision about which ones you play, does the Be Perfect role sound familiar?

Others respond by saying, "I do them *all!*" Most of us do all of them at some time. Few of us do all of them at all times. Our time behavior changes and fluctuates as much as other aspects of our behavior and personality.

Don't be too quick to put an indelible label on yourself or anyone else. We all change. You play one role at one time and a different one at another time. Pick the two you play *most frequently*. You may use the same two roles on and off the job or they may differ in each situation.

What are your two major compulsive time roles?

At Work:                          Off the Job:

_____              _____

_____              _____

Based on your own experience and the techniques listed after each of the five types, pick two or three techniques that would be helpful for you to use more frequently.

At Work:                          Off the Job:

_____              _____

_____              _____

## HELP OTHERS WITH YOUR INSIGHTS

When you understand your most frequent compulsive time uses, those around you can be more constructive in the ways they relate to you. I mentioned that I often let myself fall into the Hurry Up role when I'm under pressure. I typically combine that with a Be Strong mode. It's that old hurry-and-do-everything-yourself routine.

A long-time associate of mine has learned what to do when she sees me standing and working at my desk. She reaches over and touches me lightly on the arm. She says, "Dru, sit down a moment. Tell me the most important thing that I can do for you right now." It works every time. Why? First, the touch gets my attention. Normally I don't listen well when I'm in a compulsive time frame. Sitting down also helps pull me out of the rushing mentality. Her emphasis on "most important" is vital for someone who is hurrying. It helps me set priorities. And her offer of assistance brings me out of the Be Strong role.

Key points to remember to help you conquer compulsive time use:

- Know which compulsive time roles you follow most frequently.
- Pick the time techniques that help reduce them.
- Concentrate on using those few techniques to reduce compulsion and expand choice time.
- Every day, clear the way to enjoy more of your creative and productive choice time.

# Step 2.
## Get Yourself Organized and Going

---

## Improve Your Lifestyle and Accomplishments

# 10

## HOW TO GET ORGANIZED
## IN SPITE OF
## TOO MANY DEMANDS

Interruptions and demands are the number one time problem most people face. Demands are even harder to handle because they come from all directions, in different sizes, at every level of urgency, and in all degrees of importance. Bosses, subordinates, co-workers, family members, friends, business contacts—they all want some of your time. The individual demands may be small, but cumulatively they take a heavy toll. You can end up feeling stripped and robbed of your most valuable asset—your time.

The first step in getting and *keeping* yourself organized is to detect the hidden drains on your time. Don't allow demands to nibble away at your time without paying close attention to what is happening. Learn to recognize them, analyze them, and prepare for them. You'll take a giant stride toward putting more quality time in your life when you know where your time is going.

### SORTING OUT YOUR TIME TODAY

Every day, give yourself ten to twenty minutes to sort out what happened to your time during the day. This time will help you discover specifically what demands and interruptions you faced, who made them, how you can anticipate, prevent, or reduce them. Like the instant video replay of a football game, rerunning your actions provides insights not possible in the middle of the scrimmage.

Many people feel too pressed to set aside a few minutes a day for this exercise. That complaint reminds me of a phrase that was popular in the logging community where I grew up: "Take time to sharpen the saw." That's what you are doing in those ten to twenty minutes—sharpening the tools that will help prevent future time demands.

Carving out this time requires creativity. It's often difficult

67

to find the time during the daily routine. It may be easier to do at home, or before or after office hours at work. A retailer gives himself sorting-out time by getting to his store twenty minutes before his employees are due to arrive. One woman with considerable job and family responsibilities does it in the bathtub. She combines her daily sorting-out time with her beauty routine. She wraps her hair in a towel, puts cold cream on her face, and sinks into a relaxing bubble bath before bed each night. For twenty uninterrupted minutes, she goes over her notes in her daily calendar to identify demands and interruptions, and plans ways to prevent them in the future.

## PRESSURED? USE A D & I CHART

If you don't want to use your daily calendar to keep track of demands and interruptions, set up a Demands and Interruptions Chart in a section of your notebook. Keep the notebook handy so you can use it during the day to jot down the information you need. Whenever a demand or interruption occurs, take a minute to record when it happened, who made it, what the subject was. Use any lulls during the day to fill in more details, but those three aspects are vital—when, who, and what.

Rich G. is the special events director of a large tennis club. His demanding schedule is packed with interruptions. He decided to keep a D & I Chart to discover how to reduce them. He used 3 × 5 cards for his notes and kept them in a file box on his desk next to the phone. He had so many interruptions when he was away from his desk that he even carried some cards in the pocket of his tennis shorts. To get the sorting-out time he needed, he hid out in the club's laundry room for ten or fifteen minutes. When he went through his cards, he discovered a pattern. Most of the interruptions came from club members asking about starting time. The number of interruptions peaked three days before tournaments. He prevented the problem by posting a schedule a week in advance on the members' bulletin board. He made sure there was a copy at the main switchboard so the operator could provide the information requested. By using a D & I Chart, he eliminated dozens of unnecessary interruptions from his day and served his club members more effectively.

## DESPERATE? USE A TIME RECORD

Some people tell me that they have so many interruptions
and demands that even a D & I Chart isn't enough. If that's
how you feel, you may want to write out a Time Record and
Log. I don't stress this, because I've found that most people
won't do it. But if your time problems are especially difficult,
this is an excellent technique.

Use a time record when you are feeling particularly
pressured or frustrated. Whenever I'm not accomplishing
what I want from my time, I keep one with fifteen-minute in-
crements. I jot down what I did and number it according to
this scale: I—The best thing to be doing at this time, something that is essential or of central concern; II—A good thing
to be doing, but not the best at this time; III—A total waste
of time. The very act of keeping a time record increases my
effectiveness. I can't bear to admit that it took me an hour to
begin working on a "I," so I get a faster start.

Use a format that fits your own style and needs. Here's another example.

Jeff P., a hardworking young executive in a manufacturing
plant, felt the best way to get a handle on his time was to
plot a detailed Time Record and Log. His first day's entry ap-
pears below:

7:00–7:35    Got up, showered, shaved, dressed. Needed
             extra five minutes to change shirt and tie
             when discovered brown suit not back from
             cleaners.
7:35–8:00    Breakfast. Jonny asked if I could come home
             early enough to catch some of his Little
             League game. Linda reminded me I wanted to
             take car to garage for work on that clinking
             sound. Asked me to stop off to get wine for
             tonight's dinner party.
8:10–9:15    Commute. Missed regular bus; delayed twen-
             ty minutes.
9:15–10:15   Read mail. Pile included documents that sec-
             retary should have routed to others. George
             came by to complain about problems of office
             space. Told him to come by later. Boss called
             about Apex proposal. Promised it would be
             on his desk at 9:00 A.M. tomorrow. Data-

|                | processing department asked for delay in delivering figures I needed for luncheon meeting with client today. Vacation schedules put them behind. Spent twenty minutes on these interruptions. |
|----------------|---|
| 10:15–Noon     | Tried to concentrate on Apex proposal. Kept being interrupted by phone calls secretary should have screened. |
|                | George came by again. Maryann wanted to talk about problems with new word-processing equipment. Says it's not working right. |
| Noon–1:00      | Client luncheon. Had to schedule another meeting since did not have figures from data processing. |
| 1:00–2:00      | Tried to get Apex proposal wrapped up. |
| 2:00–3:00      | Went through "in" basket. Found several things needed immediate response. Dictated correspondence. Made three phone calls that require follow-up letters to confirm details. |
| 3:00–3:15      | George came by again. Staff meeting interrupted our discussion. |
| 3:15–4:00      | Staff meeting. Most of time taken up by complaints about new word-processing equipment. |
| 4:00           | Left office to get to Little League game. Took Apex proposal home, plus that follow-up correspondence. |
| 4:45–5:15      | Little League game. |
| 5:50           | Arrived home. Had forgotten to pick up wine; took twenty minutes to drive to store and back. That clink reminded me I must take car to mechanic. |
| 6:00–7:00      | Helped bathe and feed the children. Linda occupied with preparations for dinner party. |
| 7:00–10:00     | Dinner party. Good evening, but worry about Apex proposal kept intruding on my enjoyment. |
| 10:30–11:30    | Finished draft of Apex proposal, dictated that follow-up correspondence. Bed. Hard to get to sleep. Apex proposal still needs to be typed. Won't be on boss's desk at 9:00 A.M. as promised. |

When Jeff looked over his time log during his bus commute the next day, he knew it would help him sort out his demands. He could see where his time had gone.

## AIM FOR SPECIFICS

Begin your ten to twenty minutes of daily sorting-out time by looking at your time log and asking: "What happened to my time? Where exactly did it go? What did I accomplish?"

Now dig deeper. *When* did the demands occur? *What* was the subject of the demand? *Who* made the demand? The time, subject, person are key elements. Now decide which demands are likely to increase, which to decrease. Which ones require no immediate action? What are the persistent problems? If a demand has occurred three times, you have a trend, and it will probably occur again. Analyze and prevent.

Let's take a look at Jeff's Time Record and Log. George came in three times to talk about the problem of office space. Jeff knows this problem will decrease when the renovations under way are completed. If he takes the time to explain the renovation schedule to George, it will help prevent repeated interruptions.

The time-consuming complaints about the new word-processing equipment could stem from several causes: a need for better equipment, better maintenance, or better training in using the equipment. Jeff can investigate, then take the appropriate action.

Jeff realized that the deadline problem with the Apex proposal wasn't a one-time occurrence. It stemmed from his habit of playing the Hurry Up and Be Strong roles. He procrastinated on large projects and he hated to ask for help. By using the techniques appropriate for these roles, he can work on these developmental areas.

Jeff's secretary was new on the job. He had to tell her directly that he needed her help to concentrate on his work. She needed to learn how to screen calls and route mail. The data-processing department's delays could be solved by bringing in temporary help to fill in for vacationing employees.

Jeff and Linda often gave dinner parties. He realized he could avoid those last-minute errands to buy wine if he had the wine delivered. If he ordered what they needed for the next two months, he could get a price discount, too.

## KEEP YOUR SYSTEM SIMPLE

Whatever method you choose, keep it simple. If your system is too elaborate, it will take too much of your time. If your pace is fast, give yourself a few minutes mid-morning, at lunchtime, and again in mid-afternoon to jot down the three key factors. If you have dozens of demands, don't wait until the end of the day to write them down. The time record is very revealing, so keep your notes confidential. That way you are more likely to write down key facts—even if they are not flattering.

After several weeks, you will be able to streamline your fact-finding skills. You'll know when you need more information. You'll recognize those instances when the briefest account will suffice. Focus on the basic elements: time, person, and subject.

Daily sorting-out time takes only a few minutes, but it can save hours. When it is an ongoing habit, it can help you anticipate, prevent, or reduce interruptions and demands. You can spot those persistent problems and solve them.

## FEELING PRESSURED
## CAN BE ITS OWN REWARD

If you feel that you just don't have ten or twenty minutes to sort things out, consider what you are getting out of your present use of time. Remember the secret pleasures of mismanaging time? Being in demand may generate feelings of popularity or importance. It may provide an excuse for avoiding more important work. It could offer justification for an extended evening over martinis. If you do decide *not* to track down the source of your interruptions and demands, at least understand what you are getting out of your time.

## LOOK DOWN THE ROAD—
## FORECAST DEMANDS

Once you become adept at sorting out demands, anticipate any deadlines that you might miss. If you know someone will nag you for missing a deadline, go to them first. Don't wait until the final hour to tell your boss that report won't be on his or her desk when promised. Tell him immediately, and offer a realistic timetable for completion. Then get to work on it. You will be able to concentrate more fully because you won't be worrying. Your boss will have the opportunity to schedule productive work to fill the time previously set aside to read the report. It will also help the other staff members who might be involved. They can plan their own time more productively. They won't be caught unprepared. The organization profits, and so do you.

## PREVENT AND POSTPONE

Your fact-finding may reveal that some of the demands could be handled more appropriately by someone else. Don't respond automatically to every demand. Take a minute to consider it. If it could be handled best by someone else, refer the demand to that person.

Avoid the temptation of believing that you are responsible for everything. If the person making the demand should be handling it himself, you could respond by saying, "That's an important question. I don't have all the information for you. Let's track down the exact reference together. Then in the future you can respond to these questions on your own. It will save you time in the long run. We'll need thirty to forty minutes to track down the reference. Can I stop by your desk at the end of the day? That way, we'll be free to concentrate."

You may choose to handle a demand at another time since a few hours often won't make a crucial difference. If you do this, tell the person specifically *when you will be available*. A "talk with you later" is more likely to be interpreted negatively than a specific time. Use something like, "Can I stop by your desk at three this afternoon?" Then the other person won't interrupt you by constantly checking back. You will be free to concentrate so you'll work more effectively.

In some cases, you can defer demands for a considerable length of time. For example, if you receive a call asking you to solicit for the local community fund drive at a bad time for you, you can say, "I know it's a good cause, but I'm concentrating on Girl Scouts this year." You've let them know you aren't available this year, but perhaps you will be next year. It's courteous, and it saves everyone time.

## MORE THAN "GETTING ORGANIZED"—
## A SUSTAINING SENSE OF ORDER

Learning how to handle time demands is an ongoing process. You may not hit upon the perfect answer right away, but you will be amazed at how much relief you can get by giving yourself ten to twenty minutes daily sorting-out time. Doing this every day produces maximum benefits. Even if you do it only four times a week for two weeks, I guarantee you'll discover valuable information. You will be able to discover what your demands are, when they crop up, and where they come from. You will be able to anticipate them, and develop strategies to prevent or reduce them. You will do a lot more than "getting organized"—you'll build a sustaining sense of order that will reward you every day of your life.


## DO IT TODAY

Staying disorganized and harassed doesn't help you or anyone else. Know where your time is going. Your work will be easier and more enjoyable—and you'll be doing a favor to everyone around you. Start now—do it today.

# 11

## HOW TO SET OBJECTIVES
## WHEN YOU DON'T EVEN
## KNOW WHAT YOU WANT

Many of us don't set goals and objectives even though we understand their importance. This problem may have psychological roots, stemming from early childhood programming.

When you were a child, did you hear, "You don't know what you want," "I'll tell you what you want," or "What you want is . . ."? This type of conditioning often carries over into adult life. You can grow up with the feeling that someone else has to tell you what you want because you can't think for yourself.

You may hold yourself back from knowing what you want because you think your objective must be perfect. It doesn't. You can change your mind. As you update your wants continually throughout your life, you may find that they have changed because your circumstances have changed.

There's also a widespread myth that knowing what you want is synonymous with being pushy, rude, or egotistical. Listen to the tone of voice most people use when they say something like, "She really knows what she wants." There's often an undertone of disapproval.

Knowing what you want is a preliminary step to setting meaningful objectives. Here's an easy way to begin.

### THE WANTS INVENTORY

The "Wants Inventory" technique allows you to use what you don't want to help you uncover what you *do* want.

Turn to a fresh sheet in your time notebook and make two columns: "What I Want More Of" and "What I Want Less Of." Before you begin making a list, consider your life as a whole. Think in terms of work and recreation, business and personal life. Include ideas that relate to accomplishments and lifestyle.

Begin with your "Want More Of" list if you can. If you

feel stymied, write something in the "Less Of" column. Then, take a good look at it and see if the flip side can provide a key to something you can list under "More Of." For instance, you may want to spend fewer vacations sitting around in your own back yard. This could translate to the "More Of" column as "travel to Europe," "camping in the Rockies," "a trip to the Grand Canyon," "two weeks at Disneyland," "an RV," "a sailboat," "golf clubs."

Each time you list something under "Less Of," balance it with something "More Of." Continue until you have twenty items listed in the "More Of" column. This usually takes about fifteen or twenty minutes the first time you do it.

Now look over the items in the "More Of" column and circle those that you want most. This helps clarify and update what is really central to your life.

Make a new Wants Inventory in your notebook every day for one week. Don't refer to any previous list *until* you have completed your new day's list. Then compare it with the items that appear on the other lists. Which items appear only once? Which recur? Are you circling the same "want most" items every day?

Use this technique on a weekly or monthly basis to update your wants. It's an effective way to begin setting all kinds of objectives. Short-term objectives are easier. Long-range objectives are more important. Concentrate on discovering these first by working backwards. Identify what you most want to accomplish in life and what you want your long-range lifestyle to be. Then work backwards to discover the steps that will lead to your ultimate destination.

You won't be subjected to another sermon on setting lifetime goals for your accomplishments because these techniques cover the *two* important sides of meaningful planning—accomplishments *and* lifestyle. The following sure-fire techniques have helped thousands set meaningful objectives.

## TWO BIG QUESTIONS

First you need to answer two questions:

1. What do you most want to accomplish in your lifetime?
2. What do you want your long-term lifestyle to be?

For example, here are some possible answers:

| *Accomplishments* | *Lifestyle* |
|---|---|
| Build a house | Live in the country |
| Be financially secure | Be able to walk to work |
| Visit every major league ball park in the United States | Be your own boss |
| Sail to the South Pacific | Live alone |
| Become president of the company | Travel frequently |
| | Have daily contact with competent and caring people |
| Found a successful business | |
| Be a millionaire | Live near the sea |
| Compose a symphony | Live in a thirty-second-story penthouse |
| Rear healthy, competent children | |
| Become an expert bridge player | |
| Get a degree | |

No one else can answer these questions for you. Spend a quiet, uninterrupted twenty minutes considering them. Select a blank page in your time notebook and write out your answers. Be specific; your progress will be easier because you'll have a sharp focus on what you want. You will be surprised and delighted by the amount of information you will discover.

Understanding how your daily efforts contribute to accomplishing what you value makes your work meaningful and satisfying. *Do something toward your lifetime accomplishments and lifestyle every day. You'll feel great.*

Review and rewrite your answers to these questions periodically, depending on your personal situation. Many successful people spend one or two minutes reviewing their lifetime accomplishments and lifestyle every day. This helps them keep these ideas fresh in their minds. A sales executive revolutionized his sales volume by rewriting his answers on the front of his monthly calendar. He doesn't always change his answers, but writing them out each month etches the ideas more deeply into his consciousness. Others do it when they pay bills, or on birthdays or holidays.

## THE ONE HUNDREDTH BIRTHDAY TECHNIQUE

This technique can provide a useful perspective on long-range accomplishments. Imagine that you are being interviewed by a newspaper reporter on your one hundredth birthday and asked to name your most important accomplishments. How would you like to answer this question? Be specific. Would you like to say you'd started a successful charitable foundation? Made a million dollars? Written a best-seller? Become an astronaut? Reared two healthy children?

Here's an illustration of how one woman used the one hundredth birthday idea to solve a dilemma concerning her short-term objectives.

Susan J. had run a special camp for teenagers for three summers which involved about 300 hours of work yearly. She loved the work although the pay was minimal. Now the camp board of directors was pressing her to continue for another year.

Susan also wanted to have a baby, continue her studies for an M.B.A., and help her husband landscape their new house.

She found herself in a confusion of questions about what to do. Should she take the camp job for another summer? Should she delay the M.B.A. studies? What about the baby and the landscaping? Then Susan took time to consider these questions in light of her one hundredth birthday. What did she want her lifestyle to be like then? What accomplishments did she want to be able to point to? She realized that she most wanted to be surrounded by family. She also wanted that M.B.A. She resigned as camp director, and opted for the things that were most important to her. Knowing her long-range desires made her short-term decision easier. She was able to focus clearly on what was best for right now.

## THE SECURITY OF
## SHORT-TERM OBJECTIVES

A clear understanding of what you most want to accomplish in the long range pays off years before your one hundredth birthday. You will be in a good position to set specific short-term objectives that provide security in the day-to-day rush and keep you on the right trail. You will be in touch with your ultimate destination, and gain confidence and satisfaction because you are moving toward what matters most to you.

Use your time notebook to help clarify your short-term objectives. Write out specific answers to these questions:

Five years from now, what do you want your work life to be like?

- What do you want your job title to be?

- Where do you want to be working?

- What do you want your annual salary to be?

- What associations do you want to belong to?

- What awards do you want to earn?

Five years from now, what do you want your personal life to be like?

- What do you want in terms of family and friends?

- What do you want to look like?

- What skills and educational accomplishments do you want to have?

- What do you want your net worth to be?

When you've answered these questions, repeat the process with a one-year time frame. How well do your one-year objectives relate to your five-year objectives?

Short-term objectives can range from five years to fifteen minutes. You may be feeling so pressured that you can only think in terms of getting through the day. Write down some fifteen-minute objectives: "I won't smoke for the next fifteen minutes." "Fifteen minutes from now, I will have written the first paragraph of that report."

## THE "WHAT-I-WANT-TO-HAPPEN" MEMO

The "What-I-Want-to-Happen" memo is another helpful way to use short-term objectives. An investment adviser used this technique to increase her sales performance. She used to arrive for initial interviews with a briefcase bulging with every possible investment opportunity. But she often went away without a check in her hand and she became increasingly frustrated. Now, she composes a "WIWTH" memo before she goes into a meeting, writing out specifically what she wants to happen. "What I want from this meeting is for you to say that I am *your* investment adviser. I want to have a firm appointment to present three or four specific investment opportunities most suited to you."

The "WIWTH" memo also can help you relax more fully. Many people feel guilty if they aren't always productive, and that guilt can block their enjoyment of leisure activities. One man used the "WIWTH" technique to get himself off the guilt hook he'd created during his occasional Saturday fishing trips. His enjoyment of his friends and the fishing used to be marred by guilt feelings. He would worry about chores he'd left undone around the house and the paperwork still on his desk. Now before each trip, he reminds himself of what he wants to happen: "What I want from this time is to enjoy being with friends and have fun fishing." As he steps off the gangplank at the end of the day, he feels good. He's achieved his objective. That former guilt is gone. He enjoys himself even though the lawn needs mowing.

Pick three upcoming events in your life and write a "WIWTH" memo for each.


## UPDATE WANTS AND OBJECTIVES

Finding out what you most want and setting objectives isn't a one-time exercise. It's an ongoing process. To get the best return on your time, make it a habit to review the answers to the questions in this chapter and continually update your long-term objectives.

It's particularly valuable to review and rewrite your answers whenever you're in a stage of major transition—marriage, divorce, job dissatisfaction, career change, retirement, or reentry into the job market. Pay special attention to clarifying your objectives during these times.

How often you review your answers depends on your situation. Whenever I am going through a major transition, I review mine every Sunday. Use any timetable that will keep your objectives up to date so you can get the most from your time every single day.


## THE TIME-SAVING SEQUENCE:
## OBJECTIVES BEFORE ACTIVITIES

It's only common sense to find the target before firing. Yet how often is this logic overlooked? How many times have you heard someone suggest forming a committee before the committee's purpose has been determined? A committee may not be the best way to achieve the desired objective. Perhaps it's a job for one person.

*What* you want to achieve is the objective. *How* you achieve it is the activity. For example, your objective may be to supply a customer with information. You can accomplish this objective by several activities: a telephone call, a letter, or a personal visit. Whether dealing with a short-term or long-range time frame, you will always gain time by selecting objectives first. If you focus on activities first, you run three risks: (1) you can waste time on unnecessary effort; (2) you can get off on the wrong track; (3) you can lose sight of your objective entirely.

## USE A YARDSTICK

When your objectives are specific, you will stay on target. Here's a handy yardstick for designing specific, workable objectives. It includes the four key elements in the classic definition of an objective: result, standard, target date, and cost in terms of time and money. Here are two examples of how it works:

1. You want to increase the average order your customers place (result) by at least 5 percent (standard) no later than December 31 (target date) at a cost not to exceed $250 and sixty hours of your time (cost).
2. You want to meet three new people (result) with whom you'd be happy to spend at least a few hours each week (standard) before November 15 (target date) at a cost not to exceed $30 and ten hours of your time (cost).

If you decide on Objective 2, you'll get off track and waste time if you spend the time prior to November 15 playing bridge with old friends rather than joining a new discussion group at your church or becoming a volunteer for your favorite political candidate.

## KEEP ACTIVITIES UP TO DATE

Be firm about your objectives, but flexible about your activities. Realize that although your objectives may not change, the best way to achieve them may.

Keep your objectives up to date by taking a periodic fresh look at your activities. Analyze them in terms of what you want them to produce. Ask yourself, "Just why am I doing this?"

A personnel specialist spent a great deal of time improving and updating her files because she wanted all the information necessary to answer questions quickly right at her fingertips. Originally, it was the only way to get fast answers because the central files were kept in another building. She was brought up short one day when she reminded herself that the central files had been relocated, and were now down the hall from her office. She could get all the information she needed in less than five minutes. Her objective—getting fast answers—hadn't changed. But maintaining her own file system was no longer the best way to achieve that objective. She dumped out five file drawers and gained an enormous amount of time.

A clear, up-to-date statement of your lifetime accomplishments and lifestyle serves as a beacon that can guide you in daily life. New opportunities can loom on the horizon, and you may decide to alter course. But without any beacon at all, there's no easy way to know if you are headed in the right direction.

The action steps for setting helpful objectives are:

- Know what you want—write a Wants Inventory frequently.
- Determine lifetime accomplishments and lifestyle.
- Make short-term decisions with long-range objectives in mind. Work backwards.
- Pick objectives first—then activities.
- Do something every day toward accomplishing objectives and achieving the lifestyle you most want.

# 12

## HOW TO SET PRIORITIES
## WHEN THERE'S JUST
## TOO MUCH TO DO

$T$ime demands don't march into your life in orderly ranks, waving banners with preassigned priorities. Most often they resemble an unruly mob, crowding in at once and competing for your time and attention. Even though you know it isn't possible, they may all seem to be waving banners that say, "I'm the most important."

Knowing what has the highest priority right now is the first step toward doing what really counts. The key is to develop a flexible system you can use to assign an up-to-date priority to each demand, problem, opportunity, objective, and activity.

Every time a demand in that unruly mob calls for your attention, consider what priority it really should have *right now*.

You are the only one who knows your situation well enough to give potential time investments accurate priorities. You are the only one who cares enough about your time situation to make those priorities stick. Be firm but not rigid. You can learn when to stay with something important, even under pressure. You also can learn when to change your course. If you keep your priorities open for revision, you'll be less likely to abandon them at a crisis point.

Don't cheat yourself by saying, "It's not that easy!" It isn't easy, but it is worthwhile. Learn to assign priorities accurately and stick with them. You will make decisions faster, relieve frustration, and clear up guilt.

### KEEP YOUR TIME ON TARGET

Picturing time demands in terms of a target has helped thousands of people I've worked with. Imagine a target with three circles. The outer circle is reserved for Marginal Matters. These are the hundreds of relatively trivial demands that can steal chunks of your time each day. The middle circle contains Secondary Matters. These are the demands that may be worthwhile, but they are *not the best* things to be doing now. The center of the target holds central concerns and essentials. These are the time investments that contribute directly to what you most want in your life. They relate directly to the most important contributions you make on your job.

As you see in the diagram on page 85, the arrow is aimed straight at the center of the target. It bypasses the other two rings because you need to begin with central concerns and essentials.

## MARGINAL MATTERS—THE OUTER CIRCLE

These are the small, bothersome, time-consuming little jobs that can eat up your day: dusting the knickknacks, straightening up your desk, updating all your files, cataloging the slides of Yellowstone, organizing the closets. Many people feel that effective time management begins with these trivial concerns. They believe that until they get these jobs done, they won't be able to complete the important tasks. Not so. Work expands to fill the time available. This outer circle has the least value in terms of contributing to what you most want. That's why these jobs deserve the lowest priority. You'll find that many of them don't even need to be done at all— ever. You can do your financial planning, invest in real estate, write that best-seller, develop meaningful relationships—even if your desk looks messy and your slides aren't cataloged.

## SECONDARY MATTERS—
## THE TREACHEROUS MIDDLE RING

The middle circle is the most misunderstood, and potentially the most dangerous.

Secondary matters are worthwhile, but they won't give you an optimum return on your time investment. They don't offer the greatest rewards and satisfactions. They do not contribute the most to your lifetime accomplishments. They don't relate the most closely to your long-range lifestyle. They are not *the most* important part of your job. They are good and acceptable but they are not *the best* way to invest your time right now.

Periodically updating your answers to the questions about

your lifetime accomplishments and lifestyle—spotlighting your objectives—can help you recognize secondary matters. Your review may reveal that a demand that deserved first priority six months ago now doesn't. For example, a hardworking salesman's long-range objective is to be president of his company. His short-term objective is to acquire management experience. He is promoted to regional sales manager, in charge of six other salespeople. His first priority used to be selling to his accounts. Now that is secondary to his new management responsibilities: planning, training, and developing the sales staff. There's nothing wrong with spending his time selling, but it's just not *the best* investment of his time today.

If you spend a great deal of time on worthwhile tasks, but seldom experience the joy and deep satisfaction of real accomplishment, you are probably investing too much time on secondary matters. Study your daily time investments. How do they relate to your long-term accomplishments and lifestyle? How do they contribute to what you are paid to produce on the job? Turn to your most recent list of objectives in your time notebook. Read over your last Wants Inventory. Are your activities up to date with what you want less of, want more of, and want most? Stay in touch with how your activities contribute to your objectives and wants. It's the best way to avoid wasting time on that middle circle.

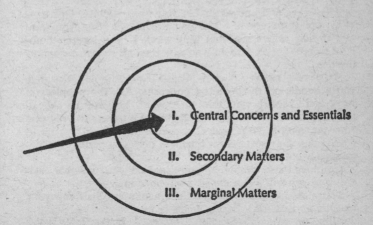

I.   Central Concerns and Essentials

II.  Secondary Matters

III. Marginal Matters

## CENTRAL CONCERNS AND ESSENTIALS
## THE BEST PLACE TO BEGIN

- Central concerns are what you most want and value in life—your major priorities.
- Essentials are what you *must* do in the course of the day to stay alive, healthy, and able to pay the rent.

Central concerns relate to your most significant contributions on the job. They are what you discovered when you used the one hundredth birthday technique. They are your answers to the questions about your long-term accomplishments and lifestyle. They reflect your deepest values and your major contributions.

Your answers to the following questions are also important signposts to your central concerns. If this were to be your last day on the job, is there anything you would regret not accomplishing? If this were your last day on earth, is there anything you would regret not doing? Not saying?

Central concerns, like so many opportunities, do not yell at you. They are quiet companions. Unless you are up to date on what you want and what others want, opportunities easily pass without a sound. You'll only sense an emptiness, a dull void symptomatic of a valuable opportunity lost. Reach out and invite opportunities into your life. Don't wait for them to yell for your attention. The relationship between recognizing opportunities and knowing what you want is close. Opportunities are resources that you can use to get what you want and to help others get what they want. If you haven't bothered to keep up to date on wants, you won't recognize opportunities.

A periodic review of your Wants Inventory will also give you a handle on these central concerns. Ask the people you work and live with what they most want. You will be able to relate to them much more effectively. You are the only one who can identify your central concerns and keep them up to date. Your daily sorting-out time will help you generate many insights about what is central.

Consider these ideas frequently, act on your insights each day, and you will live a life rich with meaning.

Many essentials are maintenance activities. Brushing your teeth is an essential. Paying taxes is an essential. Meeting a deadline on your job can be an essential. If the 7:10 is the only bus that will get you to work on time, catching it is an essential if you don't want to be late.

Essentials can be problems. They call attention to themselves. They must be taken care of immediately. However, for every real essential there are a dozen falsely claiming this priority. There is the salesperson who insists that you buy a car today because you'll never find another one, the co-worker who interrupts your concentration because he has just one more opening in the World Series pool. These demands may be urgent, but they are not essential. The real essentials cannot be left undone.

### STAY AHEAD OF THE GAME— AIM ESSENTIALS TOWARD CENTRAL CONCERNS

There are times when essentials must take top priority. We may not want to do them, but we must do them anyway. When this occurs, there's a way to increase the value of the time you invest. *Always aim essential activities toward areas of central concern.* For example, the subject of the report you must write today may not be a central concern. Learning to write clear, concise prose may be. Concentrate on *this* aspect of the task. You will increase the value of your time investment.

This technique works in your personal life, too. A father of four decided that raising children who could think for themselves was a central concern for him. Doing the weekly grocery shopping was an essential. He found a way to turn this essential toward his central concern. Every week he took one of the children to the supermarket. They learned to select items from the shelves, weigh produce, compare prices. They gained experience in making decisions and thinking for themselves. The father wound up with a lot more than groceries. He turned an essential that wasn't very interesting into a high-quality time investment.

Learn to spot essentials that may have outlived their right to the inner circle. To determine if something is still an essential, ask yourself, "What is this contributing?" and "What would happen if I didn't do this?" Spend some time every week reviewing essentials.

## CENTRAL CONCERNS
## CENTRAL AND ESSENTIAL PRIORITIES
## COME FIRST

*Knowing* what is central and essential to you is the first step in assigning priorities. Now picture that target diagram again. Remember how the arrow sweeps over the first two circles and goes right for the heart? That's because *doing* central and essential things *first* is the fastest way to put more time in your life. They *always* deserve first priority.

## GROUP EVERY POTENTIAL
## TIME INVESTMENT

Whenever you have a potential time investment, assign it a rating in the target diagram:

   I. For central concerns and essentials
  II. For secondary matters
 III. For marginal matters.

Do this for each interruption, letter, telephone call, or idea that pops into your mind. When someone asks you to do something, immediately clarify what priority the job has for them. When you ask for help, let people know what kind of priority it is for you.

Continually direct your mental energies, attention, and excitement toward the center of the target. You will feel pressures pulling you toward marginal and secondary matters. Ignore them. Learn to recognize the marginal matters right away and skip over them. Avoid secondary matters as much as possible. Give first priority to that inner circle. When you must do something essential, aim it toward a central concern.

## THE 20/80 RATIO—PICKING EACH
## JOB'S VITAL INGREDIENTS

When you feel you're getting swamped by too many jobs that are truly central or essential, there is a technique that can help. It's called "picking the vital ingredients," and evolves from a theory formulated by Italian economist Vilfredo Pareto. Pareto's law states that only about 20 percent of the causes bring about 80 percent of the results. Work on the vital few causes and you will accomplish most of the result.

*Identify the vital ingredients necessary to achieve your objective. Do these things first. You will get the most results in the least amount of time.*

The first step in applying this technique is learning how to discover what the vital ingredients are in a particular accomplishment. It isn't always easy, because individual situations differ. Here are some examples that will give you a start.

Experts have analyzed hundreds of causes contributing to the enormous number of highway fatalities. They came up with a startling fact. If we could eliminate drunk drivers from the road, we could reduce traffic fatalities by 75 percent. Just one cause has more effect than all other causes combined.

The typical clothes closet is a classic example. Most of us have certain favorites in our wardrobe—the clothes we look our best in. We'll reach for them day after day. They make a major contribution to our daily style and appearance.

Your closet may hold many other garments that you seldom wear. Some are suitable only for special occasions. Others were impulse buys that don't fit well, or just don't go with anything else. Since you seldom wear these, they don't produce the major effect of your every day look. The few favorite outfits you wear most often create that.

## ANALYZE ACTIVITIES BEFORE YOU DIVE IN

Imagine that you have just returned from three weeks vacation and picked up your mail. There's a stack two feet high. How much do you have to read right away?

First, decide what your objective is. Perhaps you only want to read the mail necessary to keep your life running smoothly for the next few days. Probably you'll have to read much less than 20 percent of the stack.

Sort through the mail looking for vital ingredients. For example, there's a card from your bookstore that must be about the book you ordered for your friend's birthday tomorrow. That goes in the "vital ingredients" pile. There's a letter from the tax board, and your taxes are due in three days. That letter is a vital ingredient. There's a colorful folder describing twenty-four South Seas cruises. That's not a vital ingredient. Put it in a separate pile. There's an offer for a magazine subscription, a notice about the opening of a new boutique next month, a brochure about a new insurance program. Anything that doesn't contribute to the result you want—a smoothly running life for the next three days—goes into the second pile. They aren't vital ingredients. Read the mail in your vital ingredients pile first.

## WHAT WENT WRONG?

One of the best ways to sharpen your skill in identifying the vital few causes is to analyze why some activity or project went wrong. When you don't achieve the results you want, pinpoint what was missing.

Evelyn complained one day that the dinner party she'd given the night before disappointed her. She'd looked forward to an evening of good conversation with friends she rarely saw, but somehow it didn't come off. She spent hours shopping, cooking, arranging the table. The hot hors d'oeuvres kept her running to the kitchen during cocktails. The main course was Saltimbocca, a dish that required last-minute preparation and cooking. Dessert was a chocolate soufflé that required more last-minute preparation and split-second timing. During dinner, she was so busy changing plates and checking the soufflé that she hardly sat down. Throughout the whole evening she barely had time to talk to anyone.

First, she reviewed her objective: a relaxed atmosphere, good conversation, an enjoyable time with friends. The vital ingredients for that didn't include preparing a seven-course dinner or showing off her most elaborate recipes. The vital ingredients were the people.

For her next dinner party, she concentrated on the guest list and kept the details simple. She made a hearty Beef Burgundy and crisp green salad. Dessert was fruit and cheese. It saved time and money, and she achieved the result she wanted.

Learn how to identify the vital ingredients and take care of them first. This technique will help you achieve more and make you feel better. That's one of its greatest payoffs. You will feel the satisfaction of accomplishing the results you want.

What are the essential ingredients for one accomplishment that really matters in your life?

Pick an upcoming event such as a meeting, vacation, or dinner. What are the vital few things you need to do to make this worthwhile and enjoyable for you?

## 80 PERCENT GETS AN "A"

In most instances, an 80 percent perfect job is all that's necessary. That inter-office memo or the weekly house-cleaning doesn't have to be 100 percent perfect every time. Take care of the vital ingredients, and you'll achieve that 80 percent result in less time. Invest the time you save on a central concern. Complete the long-range planning you want to do for your organization. Spend some joyful hours with a special person in your life.

## FEW THINGS ARE WORTH DOING PERFECTLY— FIND OUT WHAT THEY ARE

There are very few things worth doing *perfectly*. Define what those are in your life. Invest the time you need to do *them* perfectly. For the rest of your time demands, focus on the vital ingredients and do them first.

- Give every potential time investment a priority rating of I, II, or III.
- Do central and essentials first—remember everything that seems essential may not be.
- Aim essentials toward central concerns.
- Pick the vital ingredients in each task—concentrate on doing them first.

# 13

## SPEED UP DECISIONMAKING

---

When you are faced with a number of alternatives and under time pressure, it's easy to get bogged down in a state of indecision. There's a fast way out of that quagmire. It's a technique that corporations have paid me thousands of dollars to help apply. Most of us are familiar with the concept, but we frequently forget it under pressure.

*When you are spending too much time making up your mind, review what you most want to accomplish before you begin comparing alternatives.*

For example, you want to decide how to spend the long weekend coming up next month. If you begin by comparing alternatives, you can become paralyzed by indecision. You are focusing on activities first, not objectives, if you ask yourself questions like: "Shall I go backpacking? Shall I go to the country with friends? Shall I write the proposal for the new ad campaign? Shall I take that backlog of paperwork home? Shall I paint the garage? Shall I fly to Hawaii? Shall I just put my feet up at home and do nothing?"

All of these are possible activities, but none states an objective or reveals what you most want.

### FIRST, REVIEW WHAT YOU WANT

Break through that time-wasting web of confusing questions. *First, remind yourself what you want.* Then you can quickly weed out the alternatives that don't satisfy your objective. This trims your field of decision right away.

Let's use this formula in relation to that upcoming long weekend:

You realize that what you most want is a restful weekend away from home (result) on November 21–23 (target date) that won't require more than $200 and five hours' travel time (cost).

A trip to Hawaii will cost more than $200 and would eat up too much travel time. Painting the garage, staying home, or working on office projects are also eliminated. You can save time by dropping these alternatives, since they don't satisfy your objective. But a weekend in the country with friends will meet all your requirements.

On the other hand, you may decide that what you want most is a promotion and a raise by the end of November. Going away, painting the garage or putting your feet up won't satisfy that objective. In this case, working on office projects will be the best investment of your time. Here's a way to picture the process.

WHAT YOU WANT—
REQUIREMENTS OF A SUCCESSFUL SOLUTION
ALTERNATIVES

|  | #1 Hawaii | #2 Garage | #3 Office Project | #4 Weekend in the Country |
|---|---|---|---|---|
| Restful | Yes | No | No | Yes |
| 11/21–23 | Yes | Yes | Yes | Yes |
| No more than $200 | No | Yes | Yes | Yes |
| 5 hours' travel | No | Yes | Yes | Yes |

### "I JUST CAN'T MAKE UP MY MIND"

Even after they've clarified their objective, many people feel stymied by actual choice. *Which* alternative is best? How are they going to decide?

Here's a useful technique: compare each alternative with your objective *before* you compare alternatives with each other. The key lies in the sequence of steps involved in the decisionmaking process:

1. Clarify what you want most—your objective.
2. Study the situation or problem. Consider its history. Forecast its future.
3. Compare Alternative A with the objective.
4. Compare Alternative B with the objective.
5. Discover Alternative C. You make the best decisions when you have at least three attractive alternatives, so make sure you track down at least three possibilities.
6. Compare Alternative C with the objective.
7. *Now compare all three alternatives with each other.*

8. Pick the most attractive alternative.
9. Take action.

Most of us have known this sequence for years, but we often forget it under stress. Here is an example of the sequence most people fall into when they are wasting time being indecisive.

1. "Shall I do Alternative A or Alternative B?"
2. History of the problem situation.
3. "Shall I do Alternative A?"
4. Advantages of Alternative A.
5. Advantages of Alternative B.
6. Other benefits of A.
7. Disadvantages of A.
8. More history.
9. More frustration and circular thinking.
10. No action.

It's easy to see why this sequence encourages indecision. When you don't compare alternatives to your objectives, you flounder in a sea of circular reasoning, hopping from one idea to another without examining each thought clearly or logically.

### THE RIGHT SEQUENCE SHORTCUT— CHOOSING THE BEST ALTERNATIVE

The following case illustrates how one man used the right sequence to get back on target:

George R. was a young reservations agent for a major airline who wanted a career with the company. The next step was a supervisor's job. After a year and a half working the night shift, George was offered the chance to switch to days, but he couldn't decide whether or not to accept. He spent hours comparing alternatives. Finally, a friend sat him down and helped him clarify his objective. He realized that he most wanted that promotion to supervisor. Then he followed through with the right sequence of steps, comparing the alternatives with his objective, then with each other.

Night work paid more, allowed more freedom, and offered more opportunity for problem solving. George had the feeling of being his own boss. On the other hand, he didn't come into contact with higher management very often.

The day shift meant less pay, closer supervision, and less independence. But it provided greater organizational visibility and opportunities to work with higher management. He would be able to take advantage of daytime training programs.

George had a third alternative. He could stay on the night shift and enroll in management courses at a nearby junior college during the day.

By taking the steps in proper sequence, George realized that the day shift was his best choice. There would be a temporary loss in pay and freedom, but the greater possibility for rapid advancement would more than compensate for that.

The third alternative of taking outside courses emerged as the least desirable. Since he hadn't taken advantage of this opportunity during the year and a half he'd been working nights, he knew it was unlikely that he would use his free time for this in the future.

## HAVE YOUR CAKE AND EAT IT, TOO

You can use this same technique to make decisions in social situations, too. Karen C. received an invitation to an open house from her close friend Julie. The party was scheduled for a Sunday that Karen had planned to spend by herself. She needed a rest after a hectic four-week rush period on her job. Should she go so as not to hurt her friend's feelings? Should she stay home curled up in bed? She tossed these two alternatives around in her head for hours. Then she took the time to clarify her objectives. What she most wanted was to let Julie know she cared, and get the rest she needed for herself. She hit on a third alternative that satisfied this objective.

Karen phoned Julie to thank her for the invitation and explained why she wouldn't be attending the party. The day before the open house, she had a beautiful bouquet delivered to her friend's door with a note wishing her a lovely party.

As Karen snuggled under the covers until noon on Sunday, she had an added satisfaction. She imagined Julie's delighted surprise when the flowers arrived. She knew they would add to the beauty of the party itself.

## THE TIMELINE TECHNIQUE

The Timeline Technique is useful if you are indecisive about important issues. Set up a timetable for completing decisions and putting them into action, and you will feel better during the decisionmaking process. You will also make better decisions.

The Timeline Technique has five phases:

*Clarify:* Set a firm time or date to clarify your objectives. If you have trouble determining your objective, you may need more facts. Get the facts you need. Read related materials. Talk to knowledgeable people. Study people in similar situations.

*Collect:* Give yourself enough time to come up with at least three attractive alternatives, but be firm about your deadline for this phase of your timeline. Don't go on an endless data-gathering spree.

*Decide:* Write down the date for making a decision. Compare the alternatives with your objective, then with each other. Talk to people who can help you. Then decide.

*Act:* Set the date for action. Implement your decision.

*Evaluate:* After you have implemented your decision, set a specific time for evaluation. Did you get what you wanted? Run back over your timeline. It's a way of improving your technique.

The key to success in this technique is follow-through. When you complete one of these five phases, move on to the next one, Don't go back and repeat a previous one. Particularly if you are in the "act" phase, don't waver and wander back into "decide."

Choose a project that you're indecisive about. Set up your timetable and fill in the dates:

| Clarify | Collect | Decide | Act | Evaluate |
|---------|---------|--------|-----|----------|
| by_____ | by_____ | by_____ | by_____ | by_____ |

The Timeline Technique encourages fast, effective decisionmaking. When you follow the first steps in sequence, you'll make good decisions. That's what counts. You don't have to make a perfect decision every time.

## WORK WITH THE ODDS, NOT THE ABSOLUTES

Many highly successful people are plagued by a fear of making a mistake, and waste time attempting to make a perfect decision every time. This fear also paralyzes many people who are not achieving the success they deserve.

*Realize that you can fail and not be a failure.* It's an enormous help in making good decisions. I learned this from a woman I admired very much in many ways. She was very competent, secure both financially and professionally. I was amazed when she casually mentioned one day that twice in her life she'd lost every cent because of wrong decisions.

When she was just out of college, she decided to open a restaurant because she was a good cook and loved working with the public. She reasoned this would make her restaurant a success, but it wasn't enough. Within six months, the restaurant closed its doors and my friend was saddled with debt.

When she started a mail order business several years later, she was so sure of success that she even mortgaged her house. Unfortunately, the costs of doing business mounted faster than her income. After two years, she wound up flat broke.

These were devastating experiences, but each time she made it back. It made me realize that making a mistake doesn't mean being a failure.

Don't hesitate to make a decision for fear of making a mistake.

Clarify your objectives. Compare alternatives. Go ahead if you are reasonably sure it's the right decision. Don't bind yourself in the unrealistic chains of perfectionism. Take action.

## PUT WORRY IN ITS PLACE

Worry is another factor that can complicate the decisionmaking process. It eats up time by clouding our thinking. It interferes with concentration.

We all worry about something at some time or another. Money, children, health, lack of friends, lack of financial security, growing old . . . the list of potential worries is endless. Worry may be part of the human condition. Wasting time over it isn't. Here's how to put worry in its place.

## GET THE RIGHT PERSPECTIVE

If you are nagged by vague feelings of worry, figure out specifically what you are worried about. Ask yourself, "What's the worst thing that could happen?" Then rate that "worst thing" in terms of negative impact and likelihood.

For instance, you may be worried about a talk you have to give to a large group. First jot down the worst things that could happen. Then rate them according to negative impact and likelihood. Everyone might get up and walk out midway through your speech. On a scale of 1 to 100, the negative impact of that dire possibility would be 98. However, likelihood would be only 5 if you take action to ensure that you are prepared for the talk.

Someone else may be worrying about not closing a sale. The worst thing that could happen is that next month's commission check will drop $50. That may receive a negative impact of 5, but the likelihood right now is 80. Now take action to reduce that likelihood.

Ninety-nine percent of the people I've worked with find this system extremely effective. When you write down the worst thing that could happen and give it a rating, you use the best part of your thinking ability to clear up worry.

## SCHEDULE YOUR WORRIES

Another way to deal with worry is to borrow a proven therapeutic technique. Schedule your worries.

A woman I worked with was appointed head of a government agency. Most of her staff resented her appointment. There was an enormous backlog of work. On top of that, she was hit suddenly with a tremendous budget crunch and an avalanche of consumer demands. She told me that she was able to work effectively for the first six months by scheduling her worries. She freed herself to invest the rest of her time on productive action.

"Whenever I started to feel myself letting worry get the upper hand, I reminded myself of my worry schedule. I allowed myself to worry every Thursday, between 5:00 and 5:30 P.M. Somehow, that schedule kept me going."

The technique is based on the psychological reality that we control our own thinking. Many people believe the myth that their thoughts are out of their control. When you schedule your worries, you remind yourself that your concerns have value.

If your worries seem like to big a load for a once-a-week schedule, schedule daily worry time. Start by worrying between 11:45 and noon, and again between 5:00 and 5:15. Work yourself down to once-a-day worrying. Then worry on odd-numbered days. Eventually you will be able to graduate to a once-a-week schedule. Don't indulge in unscheduled worry. You control your own thinking. When you know this, you have the edge on worry.

Some worries are serious, others are trivial. Worry in itself is not a productive or rewarding use of your time. Learn to schedule it. Give it the right perspective. That's the way to put it in its place.

Choose five things you are worried about. Schedule a special fifteen-minute period during the week when you can devote your full attention to worrying. Worry only during that time.

## TAKE CARE OF YOURSELF

Indecision often evolves when you don't take care of your own needs. No decisionmaking technique can compensate for this. For example, you may need eight hours of sleep, but have been getting only four or five for the last week. You can clarify objectives, compare alternatives, give yourself a time-table, but you still won't be doing yourself justice.

When you are trapping yourself in frustrating indecision, consider whether lack of sleep, exercise, or nutritious food could be the root of your problem. If so, start there. Get some exercise, get a good night's sleep, and eat well. Then use the decisionmaking steps in the right sequence.

Sometimes a tough decision leads to insomnia. If that's your problem, here's a technique that can help. Write out all the factors—objectives, alternatives, timetable—just before you go to bed. Climb into bed and relax. Give yourself the suggestion, "When I wake up, I will make the right decision and *act on it.*" The psychological secret of this technique is the commitment to yourself to *take action.*

## MAKE FEWER DECISIONS

The decisionmaking process takes time. Don't spend that time on the relatively inconsequential matters we all face in the course of the day: Shall I have Shredded Wheat or cornflakes for breakfast? Shall I take the 8:10 or the 8:20? Shall I write a thank-you-note for that dinner party, or give the hostess a call?

In cases like these, skip the decisionmaking process. The risks are minimal; the results don't justify a big time invest-ment. Make a snap judgment and invest your decisionmaking time on what really counts.

## SEQUENCE SPELLS SUCCESS

Next time you are faced with an important decision, remember the sequence:

- Clarify your objective first.
- Compare alternatives with your objective, then compare alternatives with each other.
- Use the Timeline Technique to keep yourself moving in the right direction.
- Act on your decision.

# 14

## GET INTO GEAR AND KEEP YOUR SYSTEM RUNNING SMOOTHLY

---

Seven classic techniques provide the key to everyday success in time management. Put them to work for you *daily*. With a little practice, they'll become second nature.

### SEVEN CLASSIC TECHNIQUES FOR EVERYDAY SUCCESS

1. Do central and essential priorities first.
2. Group related activities.
3. Divide big jobs into workable steps.
4. Use a timetable.
5. Concentrate on doing one thing at a time.
6. Finish fully.
7. Do it now.

### 1. DO CENTRAL AND ESSENTIAL PRIORITIES FIRST

This technique is the keystone for building the time management system that works best for you. That's why it heads the list. You learned its value in the last few chapters. You're already ahead because you know how to put it to work.

### 2. GROUP RELATED ACTIVITIES

When you group similar jobs together, you will accomplish your objectives much faster. Here are some examples of how to do it.

You have five phone calls to make, three are essential, two secondary. Group the essential three together. Set aside time to make them one after the other.

You have six letters to write; four are essential, two secondary. Group the four essentials together and get them out of the way at one time. Do the secondary priority work as another group when you are finished with first priority work.

The existing structure of most jobs doesn't automatically provide convenient time slots to put this technique to work. Be creative. One executive estimated that he needed a daily half hour to dictate essential correspondence. He knew there was usually a lull in phone calls between 11:00 and 11:30, so he used that time for dictation. He found he often had enough time left over to tackle his secondary letters as well.

The mother of four active youngsters had a lot of miscellaneous mending to do. She used to waste time getting out the sewing box and mending each garment as the need arose. Now she groups the mending and does it once a week. She adds a dash of excitement to the chore by listening to her favorite records at the same time.

### 3. DIVIDE BIG JOBS INTO WORKABLE STEPS

Major tasks sometimes appear overwhelming, which is why we often procrastinate or hold ourselves back from undertaking them. Take time to divide big jobs into workable steps. You'll get them done faster and you'll experience an exhilarating sense of being in control. Remember, a twelve-story brick building looks massive until we remember that it was built one brick at a time. Here's how a young advertising account executive put the technique to work on his first major assignment.

Al S. was asked to supervise production of a promotional brochure for a large hotel. He had four weeks to complete the assignment. He was excited by the opportunity, but frightened by the scope of his responsibilities. He got things under control by dividing the job into these workable steps.

a. Review the details of the project: size of brochure desired, production budget, etc.
b. Assemble data copywriter needs for writing copy.
c. Present first draft of copy to client for approval.
d. Have writer make any necessary revisions in copy.
e. Have photographer take photos for brochure.
f. Take copy and photos to art department for layout.
g. Get client approval of layout.
h. Get three printing estimates.
i. Assign printer and get brochure into production.
j. Have brochure delivered to client.

When Al looked at the job in terms of the individual steps, he felt more confident. By proceeding step by step, he got everything wrapped up in record time.

## 4. USE A TIMETABLE

It's psychologically true that a timetable provides a spur to action. Setting a deadline that you're committed to meet makes it real. First decide what your objective is. Then choose a target date. Now work backwards to develop your timetable. Go over the activities that will help you accomplish what you want. Speculate how much time each step is worth. Give each one a specific target date within the timetable. Avoid unnecessary perfectionism. Use your timetable to help you do things at the best times. You will be able to act much more quickly and easily.

## 5. CONCENTRATE ON DOING ONE THING AT A TIME

Have you ever had a meeting with someone who answers the phone, signs letters, and tries to carry on a conversation with you at the same time? If you have, you know what a waste of time it is for both of you. That's why it's so important to concentrate on doing one thing at a time, even if the task requires only a few minutes of work.

This doesn't mean you can *accomplish* only one thing at a time. If you are preparing a casserole for tonight's dinner, you can double the recipe and freeze the extra casserole for another meal without interfering with your concentration.

If you want to thank a co-worker for help on a recent project and let her know you will be out of town for the next week, the same phone call can accomplish both objectives. In addition, by expressing appreciation, you create a climate for greater motivation. Your co-worker will feel more inclined to help next time the need arises. You've also saved your co-worker from wasting time trying to contact you next week.

## 6. FINISH FULLY

Make finishing fully part of your daily routine. You will get more done, feel better, and help your friends and colleagues. Completing four projects instead of leaving eight half-finished will pay off in three ways:

- it adds to your energy level
- helps your concentration
- boosts your feelings of personal satisfaction and motivation.

Being around someone who constantly leaves things half-done is irritating and distracting. How do you feel when you get a phone message that has no number for a return call? What about the book that's borrowed and never returned? The paper crumpled to throw away but left on the top of the desk? The socks lying on the living room floor instead of in the laundry basket?

Finishing fully has enormous value. It's particularly helpful to someone who has a problem with paperwork or clutter. Even if you don't feel like it at first, develop a pattern of finishing fully. You'll gain a sense of completion and calmness that can help your whole mental outlook.

## 7. DO IT NOW

Make it a habit to see "now" as the best time to do what you most want to accomplish. The technique will spur you to action, and generate an awareness of the potential of each moment. It will help you utilize every day to its fullest. When you know what you want to accomplish, use every opportunity life offers to do it *now*.

If you realize that you need to use one of these classic techniques more frequently, give yourself some extra help through repetition. Several times a day, say to yourself, "I finish fully," or, "I do centrals and essentials first."

Check your time each day and discover how well you did with each of these classic techniques. The father of time management, Benjamin Franklin, described in his autobiography how he worked each day to reinforce the same time techniques.

## DOZENS OF STIMULATING COMBINATIONS

These seven techniques are not a rigid set of rules. They are firm but flexible guidelines. Make them a part of your everyday life. They provide the freedom to create exciting new ways to deal with time demands and eliminate the boredom inherent in conventional time management systems. These key techniques can be combined in dozens of stimulating ways to help you get what you want from your time.

# 15

## A HIGH-GEAR PROGRAM
## NEEDS THE RIGHT
## EQUIPMENT

Your time is important. You deserve all the special equipment you need to make it run more smoothly. Invest in yourself. Get exactly what you need—particularly in terms of (1) a personal calendar, (2) a daily action sheet, and (3) a special place at home where you can work with them.

### A CALENDAR FOR
### CONCENTRATION AND CONTROL

Calendars don't box you in as many people fear. They free you. They can help you relax more fully and avoid worry. They boost your ability to concentrate. Most people can double their previous level of concentration when they learn how to use a calendar. Calendars reinforce the habit of doing one thing at a time, one of the most valuable time-saving techniques that you can acquire.

Our minds are incredibly complex creations. If we don't jot down an upcoming appointment, we'll keep reminding ourselves of it again and again. A reminder about that dentist appointment will float to the surface of your mind when you are trying to concentrate on writing a report. Worry that you'll forget the date of the board meeting can dampen your pleasure in a movie. A nagging feeling that you may have missed your mother's birthday will interfere with the free flow of ideas you need in a job interview.

### THE PERFECT MATCH

The best way to conquer any feeling that a calendar will box you in is to choose one that you will enjoy using. Take the time to shop for a calendar that combines esthetic appeal with practicality. If you enjoy the feel of tooled leather, buy one with that kind of binding. If burgundy is your favorite color, choose a burgundy one. Calendars come in hundreds of styles and colors. There's sure to be one that's perfect for you.

The formats differ also. Some provide a full page for every day, others offer a week at a glance, or a month at a glance. Choose the format that's best for your needs.

Most people find that a personal calendar they can carry with them offers maximum benefits. It's always handy so it can be used for social and work commitments. It can be pulled out for a quick review whenever there's an extra moment of waiting.

In general, it's a good rule-of-thumb to use only one calendar. However, large families may benefit from an additional family calendar to help eliminate the conflicts of various schedules. Steven can enter the dates of the Little League games for which he'll need a ride from Mom. Karen can jot down the weekend she's going skiing so Mom and Dad will know that she won't be available to babysit the younger children that Saturday night. Dad can pencil in the week he'll be in Cleveland. Everyone can coordinate their personal calendars with the family calendar. Put it somewhere visible and easy to reach—on the kitchen bulletin board, on top of the TV—wherever your family gathers frequently.

## GET THE MOST FROM YOUR CALENDAR

Develop the habit of looking at your calendar regularly to stay up to date with your commitments. You won't find commitments intruding haphazardly on your concentration, and you will be able to schedule your time in advance. This will help you give yourself time off *when* you want it. Check to see if you are giving yourself enough relaxing, nonproductive time out as well. Schedule the right amount of excitement for your needs. Study your calendar and enjoy the anticipation. (See Chapter 4.)

Review your calendar whenever you otherwise would be wasting time waiting. When someone puts you on hold on the telephone, use those few minutes to study your calendar. If you must wait for an appointment, flip open your calendar. Eliminate the waste of waiting.

Get used to looking at your calendar frequently. It will be easier to remember to write down your commitments when you make them. If you promise to phone someone in three weeks, write the commitment down in your calendar as soon as you make the promise. Then you won't have to think about it again until you have to make the call.

If you accept a dinner invitation, write the date, time, and place in your calendar. If necessary, jot down the directions on how to get there. Make a note to pick up a hostess gift. This is another way of making the finish fully technique work for you.

Your calendar can also be an aid in using your productive time to best advantage. One woman lists *scheduled* commitments for the day on the left side of her calendar and unscheduled priority matters on the right. She has the security of knowing she won't forget anything. She's free to weave in the nonscheduled items between meetings and appointments.

When you have a project deadline, your calendar can help. You've promised to deliver a brief article for the company newsletter by next Tuesday and you must choose the best time to schedule two hours of writing. A glance at your calendar shows that Monday afternoon is the easiest to clear. Schedule your article writing for that afternoon, then forget about it. You're free to concentrate on other things until that date. You know you won't forget, and you'll have the time you need to meet the deadline.

Many people use their calendar to keep track of business expenses during the day. If you've ever been audited by the IRS, you know how handy a record like this can be.

An architect uses his calendar to take care of small, miscellaneous tasks that don't fit conveniently into his regular routine. He groups these jobs for Friday afternoons and frees himself to concentrate fully on these things by giving them a specific time. He says loose ends are easier to tie up, and he gets much more accomplished.

## LEAP THE HURDLES OF RESISTANCE

Some people reject a calendar because subconsciously they feel their time isn't worth much. You can overcome such feelings by reminding yourself that your time is valuable to you, to your organization, and to those around you. Using a calendar allows you to help others with their time. You can tell them when you are available so they won't waste time checking back with you. The calendar lets them know you won't forget the commitments you make.

Other people resist a calendar because they fear they may become too rigid if they write everything down. Overcome this feeling by telling yourself, "This calendar is designed to help free me to have better times and a better life. I control my time. My calendar helps me do it more easily and more effectively."

## AN ACTION SHEET FOR A
## DAILY HEAD START

Writing out a daily list of things to do in priority order is another major time-saving technique, but it sets up a lot of resistance among many people. Usually it's that old fear of being boxed in. Sometimes, it's a deep-seated psychological reaction to the authoritarian sound of "to do." In reality, these lists can help you develop the technique of finishing fully. Completing the tasks listed on such a sheet can create energizing feelings of accomplishment. For these reasons it's worthwhile overcoming any resistance you might feel.

If you write "to do" lists but lose them, change the title. Call it an action sheet or a wrap-up list. Find a title that appeals to you. If your old habit for a day off is to write a twenty-item "to do" list, lose it, and then curl up with a murder mystery, write a special list. Motivate yourself by sprinkling a variety of tempting activities throughout your list. (See Chapter 17.)

## HOW TO PUT IT TOGETHER

Daily action sheets are simply a list of objectives. They aren't magic and they aren't carved in marble. To work effectively, you need to list central concerns and essentials first. Choose a realistic number of items. Don't write down thirty-five items if you have time to accomplish only five. Take a positive view as you work your way down your list. Don't dwell on the items that you didn't accomplish; give yourself a pat on the back for the ones you crossed off. That surge of good feeling may be just what you need to get going again the next morning.

If you have enough space, write your daily action sheet on your calendar. If not, clip the action sheet to your calendar so you can refer to it during the day.

## GET OFF TO A FLYING START

Many people report that their day begins more positively

when they review their calendar first thing in the morning and select items for their action sheet. Some begin while they are still in bed. Others do it after they emerge from the shower, or while the coffee is brewing. For others, preparing an action sheet at the end of the day is an effective way to clear their minds of that day's work activities. It's left on their desks, ready to launch them into the next morning's projects.

Action sheets also help those around you. When colleagues see you write their requests or demands on your action sheet, they feel secure that you will tackle the item when time permits. They are less likely to interrupt you. Your co-workers also know what *your* day's priorities are and that saves everybody time.

One mother found the system so effective at the office that she and her eight-year-old son both make up action sheets for Saturdays. They tape them to the refrigerator and make a game of seeing who can cross off items faster.

A working couple use their action sheets to coordinate household tasks. Over breakfast, they each review their calendars and draw up personal action sheets for the day. Then each selects those household chores that will best fit the rest of their schedule for that day. It's a flexible method that assures neither gets saddled with all the chores.

## KEEP UP YOUR MOMENTUM

An action sheet can help keep you going when you are under pressure. At times like that, you often pour all your energies into the job at hand. When it's finished, you experience a momentary letdown. What do you do next? What's the next priority? Your action sheet can come to the rescue. Cross off the job just completed, and without any loss of momentum, you're ready to go on to the next item on the list.

This doesn't mean you can't take a break. We all need time off during the day. Indeed, the action sheet makes it easier for you to take time off when it is most valuable to you. You don't have to settle for random snatches of time when you are not fully relaxed. You can take time off secure in the knowledge that you can get back on the track with minimum delay when you want to.

## A SPECIAL PLACE AT HOME
## FOR CREATIVE THINKING

Even when you spend the major part of your day at work, you will probably do a great deal of the planning and organizing at home. Create a special place there to do your creative thinking, review your calendar, and write up your action sheets.

Ideally, this would be a room reserved for this purpose, but in the average household, that's rarely practical. All you really need is a flat writing surface, pens, pencils, paper, room for your calendar, and access to a telephone. If you like to sit down while you work, add a comfortable chair. If you work better standing, use the kitchen counter and store your supplies in a handy drawer.

The telephone encourages you to "do it now." If you have several phone calls listed on your action sheet, do them now—before you go to the office or drive the children to school. If you have to write a note to Aunt Martha, do it now—before you get caught up in the demands of the day. If all your supplies are stored in a special place that you associate with working on your action sheet, you'll get a boost toward accomplishing what you want.

If you need extra motivation, add any implements that will help your time program progress smoothly—special colored pens, 3 × 5 cards in your favorite shade of blue, a desk that makes you feel businesslike. Anything that helps motivate you to get going and keep going in the right direction or adds to the pleasure of the time you invest is worth using.

## BUILD DAILY POWER THREE WAYS

- Use a personal calendar *every day.*
- Use an action sheet *every day.*
- Use your special place at home for creative thinking *every day.*

# *Step* 3.
## Keep Yourself
## Going

---

# A Program for
# Self-motivation

# 16

## YOUR PROCRASTINATION PROFILE

When I am speaking on time management, I often ask members of the audience to raise their hands if they feel they procrastinate. Usually, I get such an overwhelming response that I'm tempted to believe there would be many customers for a T-shirt emblazoned with the motto: "Never do anything today that you can put off until tomorrow."

Most of us are aware that many of our time problems stem from procrastination. In preceding chapters, we've learned some causes of procrastination. For some of us, it's a means of getting negative stimulation and excitement. (Remember those last-minute rushes to meet a deadline?) For others, procrastination is a response to those outdated messages we received from our parents. People who adopt defiant behavior patterns as children often wind up as champion procrastinators. It's one more way to "show 'em."

In this chapter, we're going to cover the *how* and *when* of procrastination so we can prevent it when we want to, and stop procrastinating on the things that matter most to us. The first step is learning how to chart your own "Procrastination Profile."

### RATE YOUR QUOTA

To begin plotting your Procrastination Profile, think about your Stimulation and Excitement Quota. How much stimulation and excitement do you need—a lot, a little, something in between? Do you find yourself in a breathless last-minute rush a couple of times a week? Do you find yourself dashing to make the commute bus every morning? Do you often involve others in a last-minute rush to help you meet a deadline? Do you feel somewhat bored when things are going too smoothly? Ask the people you work or live with for their opinions of your Stimulation and Excitement Quota. They can provide useful feedback.

Now rate your quota on this subjective scale:

STIMULATION                                      EXCITEMENT

_____

Low                    Middle                    High

## OUT IN THE OPEN OR
## BEHIND CLOSED DOORS

Next, consider how you handle procrastination in terms of your relationships with other people. Do you internalize it, keep it confined to a dialogue between you and your nagging conscience? Or do you grab hold of anyone who will listen, and talk about what you have to do, the difficulty you have meeting deadlines, how you just can't get down to doing what you feel you should be doing?

Do you go even further and involve others in your behavior—like the star who gets everyone into the act to help her make the curtain for each performance?

## KNOW WHAT YOU'RE AVOIDING

In addition to providing stimulation, procrastination also is a way of avoiding feelings—most often, feelings of success, enjoyment, or closeness. *Many people procrastinate to avoid the feeling they would have if they finished a task—not just to avoid the task itself.*

For example, Richard L. was a thoroughly competent executive who handled his job responsibilities for years by working overtime nights and weekends. The company realized he could handle a higher-paying position if they freed him from some of the work, so they hired an assistant for him. Richard said he felt relieved and looked forward to the promotion and the time he could now spend with his family. But he never seemed to have time to train his new assistant to take over his old workload. Achieving greater success in his career generated mixed emotions. Getting closer to his family was something he desired, but didn't quite know how to handle. He kept these unfamiliar feelings of success and closeness at bay by procrastinating.

Some people avoid closeness by procrastinating on thank-you notes. They neglect to write the note and hope they don't encounter the person. They cut off opportunities for contact and closeness by procrastinating.

What are some of the things you procrastinate about? Specifically, what would you be doing or feeling if you went ahead and did them? Remind yourself that it's fine to feel closeness, enjoyment, and success.

## THE WHEN OF PROCRASTINATION

Another factor in procrastination is *when*. Do you procrastinate most often at the beginning of a project? Do you have trouble getting started? Or do you find your resolve crumbling and your energies evaporating at the end, when you need that last big push to finish the job? If you analyze *when* you procrastinate, you can work around that critical point by reinforcing yourself when you need it most. You can even bolster each other with needed reinforcement at the required times. (See Chapter 17.)

## EARLY WARNING SIGNALS TIP YOU OFF

Next, give some thought to *how* you procrastinate. When you have mixed emotions about a project, do you suddenly get inappropriately fatigued? Do you get so hungry that you have to run out for a triple decker banana split before you can get down to work? Other typical delaying tactics include cleaning your nails; straightening up your desk; catching up on nonessential paperwork; scheduling a conference with co-workers to make sure everyone is "up to date."

Recognize the *early warning signals* that will tip you off to your own procrastination ploys. Take helpful action *before* you let them take over. You will learn how in the next chapter.

## CHART YOUR PROFILE— SPOTLIGHT "PREVENTION POINTS"

Shade in the marked areas on the sample Procrastination Profile diagram at the end of this chapter. Fill in the boxes that spell out most accurately your assessment of the various aspects of your own procrastination pattern. (Do it in a variety of colors if you want a technicolor look!) When you've finished, you'll have your own personal Procrastination

Profile. You'll be able to spot when and why you procrastinate and give yourself special help at those points. Ask your co-workers and your family to fill out their own profiles; then compare them. It's a great way to spot potential teammates for a wide range of projects—and it's an easy, effective way to get a handle on procrastination. It's the first step in learning how to put procrastination in its place.

## YOUR PROCRASTINATION PROFILE

| Your Stimulation and Excitement Quota: | very low | fairly low | average | high | very high |
|---|---|---|---|---|---|
| How You Handle Procrastination: | internally | by talking to others | | by involving others | |
| When You Procrastinate in a Project: | at the beginning | in the middle | | toward the end | |
| What You Procrastinate About: | | | | | |
| Projects that could mean feeling greater success and importance | | not very often | frequently | | always |
| Things that might result in your feeling closer to others | | not very often | frequently | | always |
| Things that mean you're feeling forbidden feelings, such as joy, ease, confidence, peace | | not very often | frequently | | always |

# 17

# PROCRASTINATION
# PREVENTION

Now that you've charted your personal Procrastination Profile, you have a better handle on why, when, and how you procrastinate. The next step is to build on this knowledge and develop an effective program of procrastination prevention. The three keys are:

1. Maintain your Stimulation and Excitement Quota at the level best for you.
2. Discover what motivates you.
3. Direct your energy. Make your central concerns and essentials appealing and exciting to you.

## KEEPING YOUR GAUGE ON FULL

Visualize your Stimulation and Excitement Quota as a gas gauge on an automobile dashboard. When the gauge is on full, you eliminate the unnecessary stress of worrying about a fill-up. If you ever had the experience of driving with an almost-empty gas tank late at night, you'll know the kind of stress I'm describing. You will turn into *any* station, even if it doesn't sell the brand of gas you really want.

The same thing happens in terms of time. If your gauge is low, you will seek any stimulation, even negative. When your supply is full, you can be selective and choose what's best for you.

After charting her Procrastination Profile, Belinda J. realized that she needed a high level of stimulation. She worked out a method of keeping her gauge on full by planning her weekends a month in advance. She made sure she had enough activities scheduled to give her the stimulation she needed. She chose a creative range of activities that included a new improvement project at work; get-togethers with old friends, tickets for a football game, and time to put up her feet and read a book by her favorite author.

Margaret M. was an auditor who traveled constantly. She got around her old stress-inducing need to dash to the airport at the last minute by building an extra half hour into her regular departure routine. She spent that time in the airport lounge writing letters to her children at college. The excitement of "talking" to her offspring more than substituted for the adrenaline charge she used to get by racing breathlessly to the boarding gate.

When you're facing a time project, check your gauge. Do you have a full supply of stimulation and excitement? If it's only half full, or dangerously low, take steps in advance to keep it full.

### SWITCHING YOUR BRAND FROM NEGATIVE TO POSITIVE

One of the most challenging aspects of procrastination prevention is the substitution of positive stimulation and excitement for negative.

A simple subtraction of negative excitement isn't usually enough. You will need to *add* an equal amount of positive stimulation.

Ginny L. supervised sales in a large chain of jewelry stores. She developed a creative solution for a time problem that had plagued her for years.

Ginny did her business traveling by car. She often "forgot" that her keys were still in the ignition, and locked herself out. She'd rage at herself while she waited for the automobile club to come to the rescue. As she fumed over delays, she'd angrily stuff coins into a pay phone to reschedule her next appointments. Once on the road again, she dodged through traffic excitedly, trying to beat the lights and gain a few extra moments. She'd change lanes on the freeway while she consulted a map, searching anxiously for shortcuts. She got an enormous amount of stimulation from the situation, but it was all negative.

Ginny thought she'd solved her problem neatly when she had an extra car key made to tuck in her wallet. But the momentary rush of satisfaction and relief she experienced each time she quickly unlocked her car wasn't enough to fill the void of all that negative stimulation she used to collect.

So Ginny went further. She added more excitement by telling friends about her clever ploy with the car key. She began using the time she saved to do things she enjoyed. Once a month, she enjoyed a leisurely lunch at the famous restaurant she used to speed by while munching a dried-out salami sandwich and balancing a container of coffee on the dashboard. She made regular stops at a wonderful craft store that she used to visit only once a year.

By balancing the void created by the absence of negative excitement, Ginny was able to change to positive stimulation. Furthermore, she found that the gauge on her Stimulation and Excitement Quota consistently *stayed* at a higher level than she'd ever before experienced. She avoided the old up and down mood swings.

## YOU'RE IN THE DRIVER'S SEAT

The dictionary defines "motivation" as inducement, incentive, something that prompts a person to act in a certain way. Many people believe they have little or no control over motivation. They have absorbed the myth that it comes from something or someone outside themselves—their boss, their job, their friends, or their family. They wait futilely for someone else to motivate them.

In reality, *we all motivate ourselves.* We may not do it in the right direction, or with the necessary intensity, but each of us is at the steering wheel of our own motivations. When you accept that fact, you are ready to learn how to motivate yourself even more effectively. During my ten years of time management coaching, I developed an exciting new psychological approach that will help you discover and use your own best motivators quickly and easily in every area of your life.

## "SATISFIED NEEDS ARE NOT MOTIVATORS"

Abraham Maslow, one of the world's leading thinkers in motivation, revealed a principle that forms the basis of this revolutionary approach. Maslow pointed out that satisfied needs are not motivators. To understand how true this is, recall your last raise and promotion. Do you remember how you went after that objective—how motivated you were? When the day finally came, you were excited. But how excited were you three or four months later? How did that now-satisfied need figure into your personal motivation a year later?

## THE POWER OF EARLY UNSATISFIED NEEDS

Over the years, I've discovered that Maslow's idea can be utilized to help develop a successful, ongoing procrastination prevention program. *Clarify your early (and consequently very important) unsatisfied needs, and focus on how the motivations that stem from these needs crop up in your time use today.*

These motivations are always in operation. We can't shut them off, but we can redirect them if they're not being channeled in the best ways. This energy is like a strong, fresh spring of water, bubbling up from deep in the earth and flowing outward at random. You can't turn off the spring, but you are free to channel its flow wherever it will serve you best.

## A NEW APPROACH TO MOTIVATION

Using Maslow's concept as a foundation, here are the steps I've developed to help you discover and direct your own motivations.

1. Accept the fact that satisfied needs are not motivators.
2. Identify your early unsatisfied needs. What did you want as a child that you didn't get enough of?
3. How do these early unsatisfied needs show up in your life today?
4. Motivate yourself to do what you want to do *now* by attaching an early unsatisfied need to a current time demand—then ride your momentum to greater success.

## HOW SOME PEOPLE MAKE IT WORK

Norman D. was a successful sales representative who struggled constantly with mounds of paperwork. When he recalled a childhood desire that had not been completely fulfilled (Step 2), he remembered that he'd always been fascinated by anything on wheels—bicycles, cars, motorcycles, scooters, campers. When I saw him at a follow-up session for one of my seminars, he told me, "You won't believe this, but I've kept up to date on my paperwork by sitting in my camper and plowing through the back orders and catalogs. I always feel great in my camper, even if it's not moving. It really motivates me to get the paperwork done. Now I'm working on a way to make it a tax-deductible expense."

Janet R. had recently been promoted to an executive position in her company. She realized that while she was getting started she would have to work at home some evenings. She carried her briefcase home faithfully, but often it just sat in the hallway and went back to the office the next day unopened.

First, Janet decided that her home office—the spare bedroom—was too small. She began checking the cost of installing sliding glass doors and a patio to create a sense of more living space. Then she remembered that one of the things she wanted most as a child was "going into the living room." The living room was off-limits for the children in her family except for special occasions. As soon as Janet understood the early unsatisfied need, she immediately stopped the contractors, moved her work table into her living room, and got down to highly productive work.

## HOW TO MAKE IT WORK FOR YOU

1. Imagine that you are five years old. You may get a better feel for what you were like then if you recall your nickname and what you looked like. If you don't remember that period of time clearly at first, make up some memories. Your mind is so creative that what you "make up" works beautifully. (The "make up" answer helps you around a temporary memory block.) Now, go ahead and jot down five things that you wanted more of when you were five. This doesn't mean that you didn't get these things at all—simply that you wanted more than you received. Give yourself five or six minutes to be creative.

2. How do these early unsatisfied needs crop up in your life today? I guarantee that they always show up, usually in surprising ways. A comptroller of a company always wanted to play with the money in his piggy bank. The owner of a $20,000 luxury car with every accessory imaginable always wanted the brightest red wagon in the neighborhood.

3. Now, how can you direct these early unsatisfied needs to help you do what you need to do right now? A writer who always loved the Sunday afternoon drives his

family took when he was a child found that the fastest way to work through periodic writing blocks was to sit and write in his car while it was parked at the curb. A woman who adored playing dress-up as a little girl got around her tendency to procrastinate on returning unsatisfactory merchandise by dressing up in her most fashionable outfit.

What are some of the important tasks that you have been procrastinating about? How can you use your unsatisfied early needs to accomplish them quickly? *You can prevent procrastination by making your central concerns and essentials attractive and exciting to you.*

Like anything new, this may seem awkward at first, but give it a trial run. You'll be amazed at how powerful this type of motivation can become, how effective it can be as a means of getting yourself fully motivated and moving on what matters most.

## THE THREE R'S

Your prevention program will be an ongoing success when you remember that it depends on repetition, reinforcement, and reward.

Repetition is part of the learning process; we all need to repeat new techniques over and over until they feel natural. Finishing fully may be a technique you have to repeat fifteen times before the skill feels "natural." The learning process will be easier and more successful when you build in reinforcements.

Make sure that you promote the most desirable time management behavior by reinforcing productive, not negative, behavior. If you procrastinate on a task, you actually make the problem worse and increase the likelihood that it will happen again. Scolding yourself by saying, "I shouldn't have done that," or, "I messed up again," is reinforcement for negative behavior. It's more effective to reinforce *productive* behavior by asking yourself, "What's the best thing to do right now?"

## REWARD AND REINFORCEMENT THE BEST

Positive reinforcements are the little things you do to encourage yourself as you tackle difficult demands on your time and energy. What will lift your spirits when you're facing long hours of hard work on the job? If you are a skier, pick up the phone and get a ski report. Take a walk to the supply room and do five minutes of clandestine calisthenics. If the specter of writing the quarterly report is haunting you, do the rough draft on your favorite color of paper. If you're going to spend the weekend painting your kitchen, have your favorite music and snacks on hand.

You are the only one who knows what will give you added momentum. And only you can pinpoint the best time to use them. Some people get more done when they add a reinforcement *as* they go along. Others work better when they reward themselves at the completion of one part of the job.

Rewards are the prizes you claim *when you complete your tasks*. They can range from time out to enjoy a cup of coffee after reviewing the first ten pages of a dull report to a weekend in the country when you complete your taxes. Or tell an interested colleague about a project you just finished. (However, don't pick someone who might be jealous or critical.)

Many people find that reinforcements are all they need to keep moving. Others focus on the reward they'll gain upon completion of each task, and that spurs them to continued action. Discover what works best for you—it may be a combination of both.

Learn to build a lift into anything you may be putting off or avoiding. It takes a little thought and practice, but it can help you finish even the most unpleasant task in less time. *Remember, though, pick reinforcements or rewards that keep you moving in the right direction*. Going to a movie when you are in a funk may lift your spirits, but it may not help you accomplish what needs to be done. Your reinforcements should be channeled toward your objectives; they shouldn't pull you off the track. Many things may lift your spirits, but for now concentrate on those that get you where you want to go.

## DON'T KID YOURSELF—PREVENTION PAYS

Sometimes in adult life we find ourselves plagued by a nagging voice left over from childhood that says, "*You* shouldn't need that extra help to do what you are supposed to do." The message *may* have been appropriate at an earlier time, but consider the problem from today's vantage point. If you had an employee who needed a periodic boost to sustain a peak performance level, wouldn't you supply it if you could? It's all right to give yourself the same amount of encouragement you'd give an employee. You're not coddling yourself when you recognize what you need and find ways to meet those needs effectively. If it works for you, do it.

Physicians know that preventive medicine is the best way to keep their patients out of hospitals. In the same way, procrastination prevention can keep you feeling good and getting the right things done. That's why it's well worth your time to understand your motivations and put them to work for you today.

You can conquer procrastination if you work with these key ideas:

- Develop positive sources of stimulation and excitement that will maintain your quota at the level that's consistently best for you.
- Substitute positive stimulation for negative.
- Identify your early unsatisfied needs and put them to work as motivators today.
- Prevent procrastination. Make central concerns and essentials attractive and appealing to you.
- Use the Three R's—repetition, reinforcement, and reward—to keep yourself moving in the direction you want.

# 18

# EMERGENCY CARE FOR
# A BAD CASE OF
# PROCRASTINATION

At one time or another, we can all lock ourselves into a seemingly hopeless time jam. When you're feeling paralyzed by time demands, it's too late for procrastination prevention. You need fast emergency care that will get you moving again, and that's what the Four Step Treatment Plan is. It only takes about fifteen minutes and has a long and very successful track record.

## STEP 1: CLEAR YOUR MIND

How do you clear your mind, especially when you're feeling down and a hundred problems and upsets are racing around in your mind? Start by writing a factor sheet. Jot down everything that comes to mind—all the worries, anxious feelings and thoughts. Do it privately so you won't feel inhibited by anyone seeing what you've written. And if you don't like making lists, don't list them—just write your thoughts randomly anywhere you choose. Use any tactic or implement that appeals to your creative side.

One hard-pressed executive adds his own special style to this quick-fix formula when he's in an immobilized state. He keeps a cigar box full of colored marking pens and a small sketch pad in his lower left desk drawer. When he gets himself in a funk, he tells his secretary he'll be available in fifteen minutes, whips out his pad and pens, and puts all his thoughts on paper in different colors.

A public accountant I know tapes a manila folder on the wall and writes everything down with an extra large soft-lead pencil she saves just for that purpose. She claims that it also releases her urge to scrawl graffiti.

A ballpoint pen and three or four pages in your time notebook will work just as well. The important thing is to use whatever works for you and to write *everything* down. You might find yourself noting some of these thoughts:

I feel rotten.
There's just too much to do.
I'll never get caught up.
I hate having to tell my supervisor that I missed the deadline.
My desk needs dusting.
The laundry is piling up again.
I never have time to take care of my looks.
I'm too fat, don't get enough exercise.
I just ate a whole box of Fig Newtons.
I'm mad at Joe for not calling me.

Be specific. Mention names and places. Who did it? Who didn't do it? What's not getting done? Within five minutes you will have a comprehensive factor sheet that includes most of your thoughts and feelings relating to your case of paralyzing procrastination. Instead of a nebulous whirl of negative thoughts, you will have concrete items that can be resolved. You will find your mind cleared and ready for the next step.

### STEP 2: UPDATE YOUR WANTS

What do you want today—*right now?* This step will help you sort things out so you can get a handle on essential and central concerns, not merely urgent ones.

If you are angry that Joe didn't telephone, you might want to talk to him right now, to be reassured that you still respect each other and can work out any differences.

If you hate to tell your supervisor that you missed the deadline on that important project, you might want to pull the project together now in spite of the setback.

If you just feel rotten, what you probably want right now is to feel great—healthy, full of energy, optimistic, in charge.

But how do you get yourself moving when you still feel barely able to hold the pen in your hand? Take the next step.

### STEP 3: ADD YOUR REINFORCEMENTS
### AND REWARDS

In the last chapter, you learned how reinforcements and rewards can lift your spirits. Perhaps calling a friend who always gives you a laugh is a good reinforcement for you. Or you may enjoy taking your shoes off and wriggling your toes in the carpet, taking a trip to the coffee machine, walking over to look at the view from a window.

Keep a list of especially appealing rewards that can renew your energy on hand, so you won't have to stop and think about it when you need emergency care. Select whatever works best and use it quickly.

Reinforcements and rewards aren't always absolutely necessary, but they can often improve results. If an idea appeals to you, use it. On the other hand, if the thought that pops into your mind is, "That won't work for me," then skip this step and go directly to Step 4. The same strategies won't work for everyone. Remember—the important thing is to feel better and mobilize yourself for action. If reinforcements and rewards won't help you in a situation like this, then do it "cold turkey."

## STEP 4: DO IT ANYWAY— THE "COLD TURKEY" TECHNIQUE

To give yourself more perspective, compare your factor sheet with the updated wants list you wrote in Step 2. Choose the items that are most essential to you *right now*. These will be the ones that almost jump off the page and say, "Do me now!"—like a report that your boss needs in two hours.

You may not have recognized the importance of these essential items when your head was filled with so many confusing thoughts. By putting them down on paper, it is easier to arrange them in order of priority.

Circle the "do me now" items. Shift them around a bit. Are any volcanoes erupting? Is the earth starting to tremble around a few? Is a previously quiet one starting to send out threatening bursts of steam? Which problems can wait until you're back on your feet?

Select up to five circled items. Write them down on a clean page in order of their importance. This doesn't mean that the others aren't important, but experience has proven that more than five can be discouraging. A longer list may tempt you to say, "It just won't work for me," or, "This is too hard." When you need quick emergency care, it's better to *do* a few important things than to arrange twenty-five in perfect priority order and *not do* any of them.

These five items make up your action sheet. Keep in mind that the purpose is *not* to make a list, but to give you a fresh taste of the pleasure of accomplishing something that is important to you *now*.

Begin at the top of your action sheet and just do it! Use reinforcements and rewards if they help; ignore that step if it doesn't add any energy or give you a boost. The important thing is to get going *now!*

## A READY REMEDY FOR FAST RELIEF

The Four Step Treatment Plan isn't something to use once and throw away. Use it any time you find yourself in a tight situation and feel unable to move forward. Inaction and passivity make a bad case of procrastination worse. Taking action on something that really counts is the fastest way to eliminate depressed feelings. This is emergency care, and it can help you out of a tight spot again and again. Put the four steps on your calendar, or on a card that you can slip into your wallet, so you'll have them at hand whenever you need emergency help.

1. Clear Your Mind
2. Update Your Wants
3. Add Your Reinforcements and Rewards
4. Do It Anyway

The Four Step Treatment Plan is not a permanent cure-all for procrastination, but it *is* a fast remedy for getting back on your feet and moving forward in good style.

# *Step 4.*
## Cope With Everyday Time Demands

---

## Creative Strategies

# 19

## WHEN MORNINGS ARE A MESS—CLEAN UP YOUR ACT

---

$D$id you ever wake up in the morning feeling tired, frustrated, and frazzled, and ask yourself, "Is it really worth it?" If you have, congratulations; it's an important question. Although it's a given that *you* are worth it, "it"—meaning what you do in the morning—may not be. Your early morning activities may be totally out of synchronization with what is most important to you and to the lifestyle you want.

Consider this example. The alarm goes off at 7:15. You roll over and groan—another morning to face. What will you wear? Is your navy jacket back from the cleaners? Do you have a staff meeting? What was it Jimmy needed for school today? Is there time to wash your hair? Oh-oh, there goes the bathroom door; someone has beaten you to the shower again. Better race into the kitchen and start the coffee. Looks like another frantic morning.

The details of this common litany of morning problems vary according to your own situation and lifestyle, but it's a theme I've encountered thousands of times in time management seminars. It's what makes people say, "My mornings are a mess. It's just not worth it."

### TIME IN AND TIME OUT

You may feel frustrated about your mornings because you are pushing yourself to be productive too much of the time. This is a common problem. Totally productive time depends on totally restful time.

"Time in" defines those times that require clear thinking and effective work. "Time out" allows you to recharge your batteries and renew your energies. If you want smooth, high performance mornings for the days when you must be "on," give yourself some "off" time regularly.

Many people schedule their "time out" for one morning every weekend. They put away the alarm clock and ignore the usual morning chores and routine. They wake up naturally, pull on a comfortable robe, brew some coffee, pick up the paper, and go right back to bed.

What would your ideal "time out" morning be like? Would you sleep until noon? Have orange juice and champagne while you wear those silk pajamas you received last Christmas? Sink into a bubble bath and eat chocolates?

The beauty of "time out" is that you don't have to plan it at all—you have a morning free to do whatever you like.

Build regular "time out" into your schedule to balance the times when you must be "on." You deserve it. What's more, you will have more energy, work more effectively, and accomplish more during "time in."

Now we're ready to talk about those "on" mornings when you must be at your best. The key to creating a harmonious environment for "on" mornings is simple: regardless of your individual circumstances, *every good morning starts the night before*.


## YOUR IDEAL MORNING—A FANTASY

During the evening, take a few minutes to fantasize about the kind of morning you most want to have the next day. Concentrate on developing a specific picture and feeling. Do you see yourself zipping around at lightning speed, or relaxing over a second cup of coffee while you review your calendar and draw up your action sheet? Whatever image you create, hold it in your thoughts as you take the next step— considering the specific questions that will turn your fantasy into reality.


## BUILD AROUND ESSENTIALS

Here's an opportunity to work on the technique of doing essentials first. Figure out what chores absolutely must be completed before you leave in the morning.

Are there any lunches to prepare? Do you have any commitments that require special equipment or materials? Will someone you're responsible for ask you for something tomorrow morning? Many a well-conceived plan has been shattered when a youngster announces fifteen minutes before departure, "I've got to have these math problems checked over."

If you are the person in your household who most wants quality mornings, you will probably have to ask others, "Is there anything we need to be doing tonight to prepare for to-morrow morning?"

You may decide your essential is a half-hour snuggle under the covers while listening to the radio for news and weather. If so, organize your good morning program to give you that leisurely time. If an unhurried breakfast is an essential, you may want to set the table the night before.

Everyone has their own individual morning essentials. Discover what yours are. Design your morning program around these essentials and take care of them first.

## A PRE-SLEEP SUGGESTION
## WORKS WONDERS

Before you go to sleep, plant a mental suggestion to help you get started on essentials the next morning. It may be, "When the alarm goes off, I'm going to have a delicious cup of coffee." If a morning run is an essential, but it's hard to roll out of bed in the cold light of dawn, you might tell yourself, "As soon as it's time to get up, I'm going to take my favorite run in the park."

## MEASURE YOUR MORNING NEEDS

Set a morning timetable by working backwards from your departure time. Add up the time you need to complete your essentials: fifteen minutes to shower, shave, and dress; ten minutes to prepare breakfast; fifteen more to eat it while you review your calendar; five minutes to get the car. Now add a cushion of an extra fifteen minutes to allow time for those unexpected last-minute demands that crop up so often in the morning. Total up the minutes and you know when to set your alarm. If all goes smoothly, you've given yourself a wonderful morning present—fifteen minutes to do whatever is most valuable and satisfying to you that morning.

## PREPARE FOR THE UNEXPECTED—
## KNOW YOUR PRIORITIES

Know your priorities in advance so you can cope with any disruption of your good morning program. Ordinarily, you may have built in enough time to watch your favorite morning TV show while you have a second cup of coffee. But the morning you discover that the cat knocked over the fish bowl, you'll need that half hour to clean up the mess and tell the children about the untimely demise of their pet guppies. In such a case, you know automatically that the TV show is not a first priority.

If catching the 7:10 is an essential priority, a long-distance phone call from an old friend who wants to catch up on the news need not interfere. With your priorities firmly in mind, explain that you've got a bus to catch and arrange to call your friend back at a convenient time.

## SCHEDULE RECURRING ACTIVITIES

Don't waste time making new decisions every morning about recurring activities—washing your hair, for example. Decide how often you need to wash it and how long it will take. Then schedule this activity and stick to your schedule. "If it's Tuesday it must be hair-washing morning" is all the time you'll have to spend thinking about it from then on.

Many people get hung up deciding what to wear every morning. They waste time digging around in dresser drawers, looking for the right accessory. They discover the shirt they wanted to wear has a missing button. The jacket that goes with the slacks they've selected isn't back from the cleaners. Eliminate this wasted time by scheduling a few minutes each evening to plan your next day's outfit.

Gertrude M. used to need twenty-five minutes to choose her clothes and get dressed every morning. Now she assembles clothes, shoes, and accessories in front of her closet before she goes to bed, and she's dressed in five minutes. Since she's not a morning person and hates making decisions before 9:00 A.M., this technique has improved the quality of her mornings immensely.

Incorporate recurring essentials into your ongoing program. Do them the night before when appropriate. Do whatever you can to allow yourself a less demanding morning every day.

## NIGHT-BEFORE PLANNING PAYS OFF

Some parents find it particularly helpful to schedule time to talk with their children in their night-before planning period. Generally, it's a more relaxed, high quality time than it would be in the morning, when Mom is putting her makeup on and Dad is fixing breakfast.

Cynthia L., a working mother with three school-age children, finds that the half-hour bedtime talk with her children is one of the best times they share.

"When I get home from work, I swing right into getting dinner. There's always a lot of conversation around the dinner table about what happened to us all during the day. The quiet half hour before bed is different. We talk about our plans for the next day. The children decide what they want to wear. They tell me about any special things they'll need from me the next morning."

"You know," she told me, "that half hour produces a wonderful feeling of closeness and calm for us all. I learn a lot about their lives and how they are feeling. In a relaxed way, we get organized for the next day."

Night-before planning isn't just for families. Those who live alone can benefit, too. Whatever your situation, make it a habit to look over your calendar the night before. If you have some special needs the next morning, anticipate them. Put your gym clothes and racket near the door if you're meeting a friend for racketball after work. If you've decided you want to take a low-calorie lunch to work tomorrow, prepare it the night before.

## GIVE YOURSELF A RUNNING START

The essentials of a good morning program include more than the physical tasks you must accomplish. We all need stimulation to get ourselves going and feeling good about the day, and most people prefer to get that stimulation in particular ways.

Diana R. doesn't like to talk to anyone for an hour after she gets up. She wants that time to think and plan her day. She told the man she lived with that this was an essential for her good morning program. He respected her style, and agreed to table all conversation until the last twenty minutes before they both left for work.

Robert M. gets his mind moving by listening to a half hour of thought-provoking cassette tapes each morning during breakfast. Beatrice Q. likes to watch *Sunrise Semester* on TV as she drinks her coffee. My own personal preference is a series of quick exercises. In twenty minutes, I feel as alive and awake as I used to after I'd been up at least two hours and poured four or five cups of coffee into my system.

Discover the best way to get the stimulation you need for

your good morning program. Identify what works and what doesn't, what is enjoyable and what isn't. It comes back to knowing what is essential for you and doing it first.

## KEEP YOURSELF FLEXIBLE

Be creative in adapting the basic techniques for a good morning program to your individual needs. Here's how one father of an eleven-year-old boy put this idea to work to improve both their mornings.

"When my wife's work schedule made it necessary for her to leave before Greg got up, I took over the responsibility of getting him off to school," said Phil B. "The first few weeks, our mornings were chaos. I did all the old standard things. I'd call, 'Time to get up,' at least five times before Greg dragged himself out of bed. I'd keep up a barrage of conversation to help him get moving. I'd advise him how to comb his hair, what clothes to wear. I'd nag him to make his room ship-shape. I'd continually remind him to hurry to catch the school bus, but he missed it about once every week.

"This wasn't working, and I didn't want to continue it. The tension was very unpleasant for us both. With some trial and error, I worked out a system that's much more enjoyable for us. Greg hates to talk a lot in the mornings, but he likes music. I put on his favorite music as I prepare breakfast. Then I call him once, saying breakfast is in ten minutes. During breakfast I don't force him to talk if he doesn't want to. I have learned to accept the fact that he isn't a perfectionist about bedmaking, and I close the door if his room bothers me. At 8:30, I remind him that the school bus will be at the corner in ten minutes.

"During the past six months, our mornings have gone beautifully. We don't talk much, but we feel relaxed and close at the start of each day. Greg's room rarely looks perfect, but he's only missed the school bus once."

This man wisely identified his good morning essentials: starting the day without quarrels or argument; getting his son to the school bus on time. He concentrated on doing those things and adapted his techniques to suit those needs. As a result, both he and Greg get what they want more often.

## TEAM UP FOR GOOD MORNINGS

When you live with others, mornings are a team project. Encourage everyone to think in terms of hassle-free mornings. Sit down with your household and discuss what each person wants from his or her mornings. Identify individual essentials. Work out a compromise that is fair to everyone.

If three people shower in the same bathroom, and one needs twenty minutes to apply makeup in front of the mirror, compromise is possible. The makeup can be applied in front of the bedroom mirror, or a special mirror can be hung on a convenient shelf.

If your mornings are punctuated by anguished cries of "Why didn't you wake me? Now I'll be late!" consider the possibility of personal alarm clocks. In one family of five, each member has a personal alarm clock. Getting up is an individual responsibility in that household, and they have eliminated a recurring morning hassle.

## THE COMFORTS OF CHAOS

Consider whether you are getting a psychological payoff from your hassled morning routine. Does it offer you a chance to yell at other family members? Does it provide stimulation and excitement? Some people hang on to the responsibility of waking other sleepy heads because it makes them feel needed and important. If you recognize any of these negative behavior patterns and want to change, select the techniques you've learned to help substitute positive behavior patterns.

Realize that there is often a relationship between your mornings now and the mornings you had when you were growing up. It's that old story about childhood programming. You may be perpetuating an outdated habit you learned years ago. Talk to people whose time management style you admire. Ask them how they handle their mornings. You may discover some guidelines that will help you break old habits.

## FREE YOURSELF TO DO ESSENTIALS FIRST

Some people worry that all this planning will make their mornings too regimented. If you don't allow for "time out," this might be true. Actually, preparing for your "on" mornings offers maximum freedom and flexibility. It doesn't lock you into a rigid system. It's one more way to reaffirm that you are in charge of your own time.

• Start your good mornings the night before.

- Measure your morning needs—know how long activities take.
- Schedule recurring activities to get the kind of mornings you want.
- Get a great start on your day—do your morning essentials first!

# 20

# COMMUTE AND TRAVEL TIME—
# CHECK YOUR DESTINATION

---

Are you a daily straphanger on the 8:19 to the city, or the guy squashed in the back seat as the carpool inches along the highway? Does your travel schedule keep you haunting departure lounges in airports around the world? Whatever your situation, the first step in getting the most out of your commute or travel time is to get in touch with what you are *now getting* from that time. Then discover your options. Remind yourself in this instance, as in every instance concerning your time, you *do* have choices. Ultimately, you are the one responsible for decisions about how you spend your time.

You will need accurate information for such decisionmaking. At least once every three months, tally up the time you spend commuting or traveling from door to door. Are you getting the return you deserve on these hours? Are you getting your *time's* worth?

## KEEP SCORE OF YOUR DAILY COMMUTE

If you invest your time in a daily commute, make sure your investment is up to date with your needs and wants. Every three months, assess your commute time and compare the benefits with your objectives. You may find that the reasons you first opted for the commute are no longer valid.

John and Joyce S. had been living with John's daily two-and-a-half-hour commute for twelve years. When their three children were small, Joyce had stayed home, doing occasional freelance writing and editing. Now she was eager to return to work full time. When she got an attractive job offer from a magazine with offices in the heart of the city, she and her husband sat down to assess their situation.

Joyce and John discovered they had the same current objectives: more quality time with the children, closer companionship with each other, more rewarding time at work. Joyce knew that the two-and-a-half-hour commute would make it hard for her to be the kind of parent she wanted to be, even with household help. If they moved to the city, they wouldn't have a huge, sprawling house with a swimming pool and a garden. On the other hand, they could afford an apartment only twenty minutes away from their respective offices. With two paychecks, they could send their children to a top-notch school that had exciting extracurricular sports and a rich cultural program. They'd be able to meet each other for lunch often. Their time together and with the children would be less rushed every day.

Joyce and John opted to move to the city. The commute time was no longer their best alternative.

Friends of theirs shared many of the same commute problems. When they assessed their needs, however, they decided the commute was still worthwhile. Their three children were much younger. Their suburban home had a safely enclosed yard where the children could play with the minimum of supervision. Janet was a potter; she had room for her own studio and kiln. Bart used his commute time to dictate correspondence and go over paperwork. Without that time, he'd often have to burn the midnight oil in his office or at home.

## COMPLAINING, COMMUTING, AND CHOICE

If you decide that your commute time is worthwhile, don't drag yourself down by complaining about it. This drains your energies and serves no useful purpose. Focus on the benefits when you feel tempted to complain. One man told me that he finally decided to change his carpool because the other three members were constantly complaining about the problems of commuting. By the time he pulled himself out of the car each day, he felt enervated, too. They were sapping his energies as well as their own.

Whenever you feel tempted to say, "I have no choice," realize that you are digging yourself into a deep pit of feeling powerless. This doesn't help you or anyone else. A more realistic approach is to remind yourself, "Although this isn't all I want, it's the most attractive alternative right now." When you remind yourself that you are doing it by choice, you free your energies and reaffirm that you are in charge of your life.

## TRAVEL TIME—IS IT GETTING YOU WHERE YOU WANT TO GO?

There are all kinds of jobs that entail regular travel time. Sometimes it seems that if you want to succeed, you have "no choice." But the real question is, what are you getting out of this time?

Every three months, evaluate your travel time. Realistically estimate how it *now* relates to what you most want in life and to your long-term lifestyle. Go over your list of central concerns. Does the travel time pay off in terms of these things?

Bob H. made a major job change after going over the exercise several times. Bob headed a project team doing market research and new product planning. Work with test groups and laboratories all over the country meant travel four weeks out of every five. "I was excited about my job, but I didn't feel comfortable talking about it enthusiastically at home. My wife was great. She never complained about being left alone so much with our two small sons, but I knew she wasn't happy about it. The last straw for me came one Sunday night, as I was preparing to leave again for a week. I picked up my five year old. As he'd done several times previously, he pulled away from my hug. I put him down, got on my knees, and cupped his chin in my hand. I saw two tears sliding down his cheeks. The sight of those tears stayed with me all week. I kept asking myself, 'Is this job what's most important to me now?' By the time I got home that Friday, I had decided it wasn't. My children will be small only once. I knew I wanted to be with them during that time.

"The project was coming to a close. I was able to get transferred to a field job where I had more time with my family. That was five years ago. Whenever I look at one of my sons, I know I made the right decision."

## TURNING "ON" TO THE COMMUTE

Every month, calculate how many hours you poured into travel. Include the time spent in preparation, departure, return, and recovery. You may decide it's not worth it. On the other hand, if you decide it's the best alternative for now, focus on how to get the most out of it by turning it into high quality "time in."

First, look at how much time is involved in your travel or commute. Half an hour? Forty minutes? Two hours? Block out various projects on your action sheet that could fit into your commute time. Use it for job-related reading, scheduling and planning with your calendar, assessing the day's activities and time use. Study your demands and interruptions chart (see Chapter 10) to uncover any repetitive time problems you need to prevent. Add to your feelings of satisfaction on the way home by picking out at least ten accomplishments that involved effective time use during that day. If you don't want to, you don't have to get involved in the pinochle game or the football replay during *every* commute. You can choose how to spend that time.

## A LITTLE UPBEAT TRAVELING MUSIC

Have you ever come to grips with the *unnecessary* pressures that travel can generate, especially the preparation rush so many travelers accept as part of the package? If you travel extensively, continually look for ways to shorten the preparation time. Use a checklist for packing. Choose clothes that wear well and won't require a great deal of extra care. Get a reliable travel agent. Buy an extra set of basic supplies such as toiletries and a hair dryer and leave them in your suitcase. Prepare the items that you want to take in advance so they will be ready and easily accessible. You'll save time, and be able to concentrate fully and effectively on the task without worrying about forgetting something.

Don't add any additional pressures to travel time. How often have you observed people surging into the aisles as soon as a plane lands? They jostle hurriedly toward the exit, only to wait around until the baggage carrousel spews out their luggage. Don't rush when it's not absolutely necessary.

## YOUR QUARTERLY CHECKUP

1. Take a few minutes and figure out just how much time you spent commuting and traveling the last three months.

    *commute*                                    *travel*

    _____          _____

Keep these figures in mind as you answer the following questions.

2. What do you get out of this?

| *commute* | *travel* |
|---|---|
| a. _____ | a. _____ |
| b. _____ | b. _____ |
| c. _____ | c. _____ |
| d. _____ | d. _____ |

3. Are the benefits worth the time investment in terms of the accomplishments and lifestyle you most want?

_____

_____

4. If not, what are some alternatives?

_____

_____

5. What can you do to make your commute and travel time more rewarding?

| *commute* | *travel* |
|---|---|
| _____ | _____ |
| _____ | _____ |
| _____ | _____ |
| _____ | _____ |

## GOING FIRST CLASS

Make the quarterly checkup a habit. Commuting and travel

may be part of your life, but you *can* eliminate or reduce that time if you decide it's not the best alternative right now. Every week or so, find a new, creative way to get more from this time. Make all your commuting and travel rewarding "time in." If you've chosen to commute and travel, don't waste your time complaining. Go in first-class style.

# 21

# EARLY EXCITEMENT BEATS
# RUNNING LATE

Many people who are constantly late suffer real agonies trying to be on time. They want to meet their deadlines, get to the bus stop early, avoid being the last to arrive for important meetings. But they feel they have so many demands that it's hopeless.

If this is one of your problem areas, take heart. You can learn some simple, effective techniques that will help you meet your commitments early, with time to spare.

## PICK YOUR FOCUS POINTS

First, take a look at your weekly calendar. Select one important commitment on each day that you might not meet on time. Right now, pick only essentials. Once you've absorbed these techniques, you can easily use them for less important matters. Now let's take a look at a sample week's list.

Monday your department has its weekly staff meeting. Everyone reports on individual progress, and discusses departmental problems and objectives. You are often late, and you know it's not to your career advantage to acquire a reputation for lateness. Make this your first focus point.

Tuesday you have an employee counseling meeting that you're not looking forward to. Focus on this as something you are going to be early for this time.

Wednesday your monthly expense report is due. You haven't even begun to prepare it. It's always hard for you to get that report on your boss's desk on time. This is a good item to focus on.

Thursday evening you've got a date for racketball. You love the exercise and value the friend you play with, but you have often been late for these dates in the past. This shortens the time you have to enjoy the game, because the courts only can be reserved for one hour. It irritates your friend and disappoints you both. Make the racketball date Thursday's focus.

Friday is special. You've arranged to take the day off to be a member of your favorite cousin's wedding party. You are eager to see all your friends and relatives, but you have some mixed emotions as well. Aunt Harriet always scolds you for not writing more often. Uncle Abe always drinks too much and tells the same tired old jokes. You promised to make it to the church on time, but you know it will be a real struggle to arrive before the strains of *Lohengrin* begin to peel forth. Make this Friday's focus.

## DON'T TRY TO BE ON TIME

Use your focus points to start designing a timetable that will help you meet your important commitments *early*. If you have problems being late, don't try to be on time. "Early" is the idea to concentrate on. Being on time is not enough; give yourself time to spare. It's a cushion against last-minute emergencies.

## WORK BACKWARDS

Let's apply the working backwards technique to that monthly expense report due Wednesday. You know your boss likes it on his desk by 3:00 P.M. Set a target of 2:30 so you'll have a half hour to check over the final draft and make copies. Working backwards, sort out the steps necessary to produce the finished report. Since you are just learning this technique, write the steps down to fix them in your mind. When it becomes second nature through practice, you'll be able to sort them out mentally. For now, you might write down:

- Finished report with three copies
- Overall total figures
- Total figures for individual categories
- Receipts arranged chronologically in separate categories
- Receipts arranged chronologically
- All expense receipts assembled in one pile

Remember that large projects can be accomplished faster when they are divided into smaller, more manageable steps. For big jobs, estimate how long a step will take, total the time, and subtract from the target time. You will accomplish more when you give smaller steps a deadline. In fact, you may move ahead so quickly that you'll finish ahead of your timetable. If you've targeted Monday noon to complete the first three steps, but finish by 11:15, use that forty-five minutes to get a head start on the remaining steps. Give yourself a double helping of congratulations when you do this. Invite someone who is interested in your efforts to overcome the lateness habit to congratulate you, too.

## EARLY EXCITEMENT WINS THE PRIZE

You can design an effective timetable and stick to it more easily if you create excitement for being early and reward and reinforce your desirable behavior. This compensates for the storehouse of negative stimulation and excitement that being late offers. Know your Stimulation and Excitement Quota. (See Chapter 3.) Be creative in designing and delivering enough excitement to meet that quota. Make sure it exceeds the negative stimulation you got from being late.

For example, spend ten minutes reading that favorite mystery novel whenever you're ten minutes ahead of your schedule. Motivating yourself to be early is more important now than maintaining totally productive time. If you are ready to leave for work early, don't spend those extra minutes taking out the garbage; listen to some music you enjoy. Turn on the TV to catch a few minutes of a lively talk show. Do something that is appealing and pleasurable. This rewards and reinforces your new behavior.

Let's use these techniques for that Friday wedding. The ceremony is scheduled to begin at 11:00 A.M., but Cousin Linda wants everyone in the bridal party to arrive at the church no later than 10:15. Depending on traffic, it will take twenty to thirty minutes to drive from your house to the church. Add a cushion of fifteen minutes and set a departure time of 9:30. Getting up, having breakfast, getting dressed and ready to leave will take an hour and a half. Set the alarm for 8:00. You now have a basic timetable, but it's pretty stark. There's no real excitement for being on time, let alone early. What might you do to inject some early excitement? Perhaps an old friend whom you haven't seen in years is coming to the wedding, and you'd like to have an intimate talk. Since the reception won't offer much opportunity for that, phone your friend and arrange to meet at the church at 9:30. Revise your morning schedule so you'll have plenty of time to visit. You'll be early for your commitment, and your friend will get a choice seat.

## GIVE YOURSELF A BLUE RIBBON

Make being early rewarding. Found time is like found money. Don't put it into your everyday budget; spend it on something you enjoy. Think about all the things you'd like to do if you had an extra ten minutes each morning, or a half hour in the evening, or just a few minutes here and there during the day. Have some ideas ready, so you can give yourself an enjoyable reward whenever you are early.

Jerry J. likes to memorize poetry. He carries the poems he wants to learn to all his appointments. When he's early, he rewards himself by reading over favorite lines.

A busy executive with a large downtown bank departs for work thirty minutes earlier than he used to. He rewards himself by walking to the office. He enjoys the exercise, and he can think and plan as he strides briskly along. He arrives in a much more cheerful, productive frame of mind that he did when he used to squeeze himself onto a crowded, stuffy bus for a ten-minute ride every morning.

Reinforce positive behavior by reminding yourself what you gain by being early. Share your triumphs with someone on your support team who is interested in your progress.

## CONCENTRATE ON DEPARTURE TIME

Focusing on your departure time is another very useful technique for conquering the lateness habit. For example, if you have a meeting across town at 3:00 P.M., figure out what time you must leave your home or office to arrive there a few minutes early. Focus on that time.

Your calendar is particularly useful in such cases. As soon as you enter a meeting or commitment, write your departure time above it. If you need an extra reminder, circle the departure time in a bright color. As you jot it down, take the thought one step further. Picture yourself leaving confidently at the appointed time. See yourself arriving at your destination calm and collected, with a few minutes to spare.

While you have your calendar in hand, also note what papers or materials you need for the meeting. If you can, take a few minutes to assemble those papers immediately. Tuck them into a file for that event. One man who always forgets important files now stacks them on the floor by his door at least an hour before departure.

Beware of the "one last thing" syndrome. Well before your departure, ask yourself, "If I were to do one last thing, what would it be?" Do it immediately or jot it in your calendar to do at a specific time.


## COMBINE AND CONQUER

Now, let's use all these techniques for that Monday staff meeting. First, set a departure time. The meeting is at noon, and it will take five minutes to get to the tenth-floor conference room. Since the elevators are usually crowded at that time, give yourself an extra five minutes in case you have to wait for an elevator. Enter and circle that departure time of 11:50 in your calendar. Then, work backwards and list the items you'll need:

- Notes on your projects.
- Memo from your boss on the department's monthly objectives.

Assemble the papers on Friday before you leave the office, or first thing Monday morning to avoid any last-minute preparations. Imagine how relaxed and confident you'll feel as you walk into that meeting on time and prepared.

If you are concerned that people will think you don't have enough to do if you are early, deal with this directly. Find a creative way to let them know what you are accomplishing without falling into the old lateness habit. Talk about projects you've completed. Give others information that provides clear and direct evidence of your contribution to the organization.


## IMITATE THE EARLY BIRDS

Learn from people who are habitually on time. Many won't be able to give you specific advice; they'll just say, "It's using common sense." But pay attention to their actions. How do they talk about departure time? How do they get themselves ready? Figure out how you can adapt their successful techniques to your own personal time management style. It's amazing how many useful ideas you can learn by studying people who have already mastered a sticky problem.

## WHAT'S REALLY BEHIND LATENESS

During the week, keep track of your own behavior. Analyze why and how you are late. Do you feel compelled to do "just one more thing"? Is it negative stimulation and excitement? Are you looking at every project as an enormous, time-consuming task rather than sorting it out into manageable steps?

Remember the secret payoffs of mismanaging time. Are you getting attention, secret power, getting even with someone, or avoiding a certain feeling? (See Chapter 4.) Occasionally, deeper motivations may be involved. This was true in my case.

For years I struggled to be on time. Friends and colleagues frequently had to wait for me, often on windswept street corners, and they were justifiably irritated. I recently learned that I made myself late habitually to avoid feeling abandoned.

The insight dawned one morning a few years ago, when I was scheduled to speak to a group of M.B.A. candidates. On this occasion, I was ready ten minutes before a colleague was to come by and pick me up. It was a beautiful, sunny morning so I waited outside. I stood feeling the warmth of the sun, enjoying the slight breeze, and congratulating myself on being early. I reveled in that ten minutes of rare early time, but when my colleague failed to show up at eight o'clock, I began to feel uneasy. By 8:10, I had looked at my watch at least fifteen times. By 8:30, I began to feel frightened.

The feelings weren't current; they resembled the sinking sensation in the pit of my stomach that I used to have on dreaded occasions when I was in grammar school. When my classmates chose teams for softball games, I was usually the last one to be picked because I was near-sighted, shy and overweight. I hated standing there alone until one of the team captains would say to the other, "You take Faith Drucilla."

Years later, waiting in the sunshine, I was reliving those old feelings of being unwanted and left out. Suddenly, I realized that being late was a way of avoiding stiuations where I might feel that way again. Once I recognized my feelings, I could deal with the old fear more effectively.

If you are repeatedly late, there's probably a significant reason for your habit. Discover what it is. Allow yourself to understand what you gain. You will be able to change, and deal with your time more effectively today.

## GET THERE IN YOUR OWN GOOD TIME

You can kick the lateness habit when you:

- Gear yourself to being early.
- Work backwards.
- Inject early excitement.
- Concentrate on departure time.
- Combine and conquer.

# 22

## BREAK FREE OF TIME YOU WASTE WAITING

---

Those of us who have managed to avoid the lateness syndrome still have to deal with it in others, and we're all familiar with the frustrations of waiting. We complain about it bitterly, but a solution often seems elusive. However, there are ways to eliminate and reduce waiting time, and you can learn how to deal with other people's lateness habits.

In some cases, the cause of lateness can be "accidental"—a traffic jam; a malfunctioning alarm; a bus that was late; a previous appointment that ran over or began late. Some of us fail to gauge our time realistically and try to cram too many appointments into a day's schedule.

In some instances people are kept waiting as a matter of policy. Knowingly or unknowingly, making others wait can be a demonstration of power. It can provide a sense of secret control.

For example, the president of a large company schedules weekly meetings with key staff members every Monday at 7:30 A.M. Those people have to cut short any out-of-town weekends, and must be up and moving earlier than usual to make the Monday meetings on time.

Roughly once a month, the president will be half an hour late. He always has some explanation, and he always apologizes. Although he doesn't deliberately arrive late on these occasions, it is actually an indirect way to flaunt his control over the members of his management group. They may seethe with frustration as they wait, but they have to sit there until he shows up.

Waiting is a growing problem. It's one of the symptoms of a mass society struggling to cope with increasing service demands. It's also symptomatic of a burgeoning epidemic of disrespect for the time of others. When other people are careless about their time, it cuts into your time and energy.

## FIGHT BACK

Although waiting may be a fact of life, wasting time while waiting is not. Confront this insidious problem head on with this three-step strategy:

1. Anticipate waiting times and prepare to deal with them.
2. Aim to eliminate or reduce waiting times.
3. When you cannot eliminate or reduce them, use waiting time to work on something that counts for you.

### *STEP 1:* ARM YOURSELF AGAINST WAITING

If you analyze your waiting periods, you'll probably discover that they fall into patterns. Anticipate and prepare for these possible problem areas.

George R.'s boss was notorious for running late on appointments with his staff. George felt that cooling his heels with the rest of the gang waiting to enter the inner sanctum wasn't appropriate. The company was the loser if he did because that kind of waiting wasn't productive. He devised a better way to deal with this chronic problem.

Whenever George has an appointment with his boss, he is fully prepared by departure time, but he doesn't leave his office without calling ahead to find out if the boss is on schedule. If his boss is running late, George asks the secretary to buzz him when the preceding appointment is ending. When he gets the signal, he leaves immediately. During his waiting time, George deals with tasks that don't require serious concentration, so he can drop them quickly. He reviews his calendar, jots down phone calls to make later in the day, dictates routine correspondence, or checks his current reading file to catch up on industry news.

If you find yourself in a similar situation, but can't spend your waiting time in your office, there's an alternative solution. Bring some portable work with you to the appointment and do it while you're waiting. It could be an article you want to read, a report you want to edit, some figures you want to go over. Don't waste time fuming over delays. Look ahead. Anticipate enforced waiting time. Many people who develop this pattern find that they look forward to the "extra" minutes they gain during the day's waiting periods.

Learn the habit of confirming appointments the day before.

It takes only two or three minutes to call, and if you avoid one no-show or mix-up a week, it's well worth your time.

When you are reviewing your upcoming weekly commitments, speculate on the amount of time you will probably have to wait in specific instances. Give yourself an extra cushion between appointments to compensate for waiting time. If you prepare for and anticipate these times, you can handle them more easily and productively.

## STEP 2: ELIMINATE WHAT YOU CAN

Consciously aim to eliminate or reduce waiting time every week. For example, consider an area like personal services. Do you spend time waiting to get your hair cut? Do you have to wait for the dentist regularly, even though you have a firm appointment? What about getting your car serviced? There are so many areas where we can't reduce or eliminate waiting time that it pays to explore every area where we can.

First, consider finding another supplier for the personal service. If you can't solve the problem this way, there are other techniques that can reduce or eliminate waiting time.

You have a noon appointment with the dentist and your departure time is 11:30. Before you set out, phone the dentist's office to check if he's running on time. If not, ask when he will be ready to see you and adjust your departure time accordingly.

If your staff meetings have been running late for weeks because one person always barges in twenty minutes late, you could let the chairperson know your feelings directly. "The last four meetings ran overtime because they didn't begin on schedule. This is creating a lot of time pressures for me. Will you let people know the meetings will begin on the dot of the appointed hour and then go ahead and start, even if everyone hasn't arrived? I'll support you enthusiastically if you take this action."

You can often wipe out waiting time when you let people know directly and tactfully what you want.

## STEP 3: MAKE THE BEST OF THE REST

When you cannot eliminate or reduce waiting time, learn how to make the most of it.

When you're in a "time in" mode, carry a supply of essential work. Don't use waiting time to work on secondary matters; make sure your work relates to something that counts most for you at that moment. It could be anything portable: a copy of the *Wall Street Journal;* an article on a new production technique; the phone calls listed on your daily action sheet. Even if you have only three or four minutes, a supply of work to fill that gap will turn wasted time into quality time.

If someone is making you wait, don't fall into the trap of feeling frustrated or angry; accomplish something toward your objectives instead. It's a creative way to get even with the person who's making you wait. Next time you're in such a situation, note the way in which the latecomer says, "I'm sorry I kept you waiting." Often this is accompanied by a smile. That's the tip-off. Although part of that person may be genuinely sorry, another part is happy because he or she has the feeling of control. You can then reply, "Oh, I was wrapping up some important work."

## THE PARTY'S OVER

When you are hosting a dinner party or social gathering, you may sometimes find yourself waiting for everyone to leave. It was a wonderful party, but now the evening is on the wane. You want to clean up and do the dishes before midnight, but your guests linger on.

Surprisingly, telling your guests when to go home is one of the most gracious things you can do as a host. Many people find it difficult to be the first to leave a party and welcome leadership in this area.

One technique is to begin talking about the evening in the past tense. "It was so nice to see you all. I hope we can get together again soon. It was such fun to have you over."

Another alternative is to let people know the approximate departure time when you invite them. "Cocktails from four to six." "Dinner from seven to ten." "Could you come for dinner at six thirty? We can spend two or three good hours together."

Monty P. decided that he wanted his evening social engagements to end by 10:00 P.M. If he's at someone else's house, he thanks his host and leaves. If he has guests in his own house, he goes to a nearby light switch at 10:00 P.M. and switches it off and on a few times. His friends know that's the signal for "Good night." New acquaintances are sometimes a bit surprised, but Monty does it with such a pleasant and reasonable smile that they accept it. Many secretly admire his style. And there's no doubt about where he stands.

## WIN THE TWENTY-FIFTH HOUR

We can't eliminate all daily waiting time, but we can learn to use it creatively and productively. Part of the secret lies in your attitude. Imagine waiting time as precious minutes in the magical "twenty-fifth" hour.

Maria C. works for a large midwestern department store chain. She gets so much done that she's often been accused of stealing a twenty-fifth hour from somewhere. She told me her secret. She uses *every second* to her advantage. If she has to wait for a bus, she mentally reviews her time for the next day and groups any related commitments and objectives. She may realize that her 3:00 P.M. appointment will put her in the same building as her lawyer. He'd asked her to drop by next time she was in the area to sign a couple of papers so she can group this errand with the three o'clock appointment. Her 11:00 A.M. meeting is being held near her favorite French restaurant so she can phone a friend to meet her there for lunch.

By looking ahead and noting patterns, she is able to group individual tasks into efficient time blocks. She's also better prepared to deal with any waiting time that could crop up. The minutes she gains add up to that magical "twenty-fifth" hour. If you use the techniques for creative waiting, you'll be able to have that hour too.

# 23

## SHOPPING AND HOUSE-WORK—PROGRAMS VERSUS PROJECTS

*H*ousework and shopping are chores that almost all of us have to face. Whether you're a desert nomad with a tent to fold each dawn, or a city-dweller with a ten-room condominium to care for, somebody is responsible for keeping the place liveable, finding food and clothing, and bringing all these necessities together. If that includes you, read on.

### DON'T HESITATE TO GET HELP—YOUR TIME IS WORTH IT

First, consider whether you want to employ help. Juggling the demands of a career and a household, even with family help, is difficult. Take a moment to consider the value of your time per hour (whether in dollars or in "psychic pay") versus the cost of professional help for these tasks. There are an enormous number of skilled people available to serve you by the hour for a fair fee. Don't hold yourself back by believing that your time is not that important.

### FUNCTIONAL SHOPPING—WRAP IT UP IN RECORD TIME

First, let's consider shopping. Recreational shopping can be a delightful diversion. Browsing for sheer pleasure appeals to many of us as a lovely way to spend a half hour or more of "time out." That's not the kind of shopping that presents problems. We're talking about functional shopping—acquiring the necessary boxes of laundry detergent, cans of soup, socks, and shirts. You can combat this time demand several ways.

The best and most expensive way is to hire shoppers and consultants. This is one of my favorite indulgences, but it's not always a luxury. In many instances, it's turned out to be a money saver, too.

Several years ago I met a woman who runs a "need-a-wife" service, providing shopping and household assistance. She prepares parties, and shops for furniture, by making comparative studies and presenting a folder full of options listing advantages and costs of each piece. Once a decision is made, she arranges the actual delivery.

This woman is a superb example of someone who turned her talents and experience into a profitable activity once her children were grown. Because she can shop for several clients at one time, she is able to provide the service at reasonable rates and still make it worthwhile for herself.

Another way to handle functional shopping is to patronize stores that deliver. Consider the extra cost of delivery and decide if it's equal to or less than the value of your time.

The wardrobe consultant that I work with has been a real boon. I used to buy items at random, often shopping hurriedly in airports. I'd buy pieces that didn't add up to a coordinated look, and would end up in back of the closet with the rest of the inactive 80 percent of my wardrobe. (See Chapter 12.) It was an expensive way to shop. If shopping for clothes takes too much of your time, you probably will find it worthwhile to hire such a consultant. They know the stores that carry lines that are best for you, and can get in and out of stores quickly. They will offer the candid advice that a friend or salesperson might avoid. It's a rapidly growing profession, so you'll find a number of people you can experiment with. If one doesn't suit your style, find another.

Choose a shopping schedule that best meets your needs. Spring and fall shopping trips are sufficient for mine. These two regular trips save me dozens of hours of strictly functional clothes shopping.

## SHOPPING SHEETS—
## STANDARDS AND SPECIALS

Now let's consider household shopping. If you learn how to group the related items you need to keep the home fires burning brightly, you'll be able to save many hours. You can start by learning how to use standard and special shopping sheets.

First, list all the standard items you need each week—milk, bread, eggs, for example—then figure out the amounts you generally use. What other items do you end up buying weekly? Estimate a week's worth of all these recurring items and enter them on your standard weekly shopping list.

It's not necessary to make a completely new list each week, just add any changes to your standard list, or make the changes on a separate page. You can even keep the list in your calendar and make any revisions as you push your cart between the rows. It will vary according to sales and seasons, but a standard list will eliminate those bothersome trips for just one item.

Often, shopping for special items eats up unnecessary time—a light for the oven, extra hooks for the coat closet, a particular nut or bolt. First, write down all these special items you need on one sheet. As soon as the need for an item occurs to you, jot it down. Keep this special shopping sheet in your calendar or wallet. As soon as you realize that you're going to need a gift, new office supplies, a book, etc., add it to the special shopping sheet.

Once a week, spend fifteen minutes looking over the sheet and *group related kinds of purchases*. For example, all drugstore items go in one group. When I make my monthly trip to a drugstore, I move quickly through all the departments, picking out what I need and use less than half the time it formerly took.

You can save even more time by purchasing a three-month supply of basic staples. Most of us can store that amount of paper goods, light bulbs, and canned goods in our home, eliminating the need for multiple trips.

Jim P. started keeping house for himself after his divorce, and was amazed at the amount of time it took. "I never knew housekeeping was so time-consuming. The light in the hallway would burn out. I might remind myself about it for three days before going to the store for a replacement. I finally realized I would always need light bulbs, and began buying several months' supply in advance."

You may not need to purchase everything on your special shopping sheet right away. But writing the items down assures you that you won't forget them. You can also use those odd moments when you're early or waiting to look over your shopping sheet and see if there are any particular things you can pick up during the day.

1. Write all your special shopping needs on one sheet. Don't use dozens of miscellaneous slips of paper.
2. Enter the item as soon as you realize you need it.

3. List staples in amounts to serve you for a three-month period.
4. Read over your special list at least once a week. Group related purchases.
5. When you have crossed off most of the items, recopy your list on a fresh sheet.

## CAPITALIZE ON START-UP TIME

Remember the benefits of grouping related activities? (See Chapter 14.) You can use this technique successfully for housework and capitalize on the energy you need to begin your chores.

For example, the living room must be vacuumed after last night's party. You have to take out the vacuum, unwind the cord, plug it in, and switch it on before you begin. Why not capitalize on this start-up time and whiz through the entire apartment while you have the vacuum out and are revved up and ready to go? Use the momentum you've already built up.

A working couple used the grouping technique when they could make their day more attractive into the bargain.

Sarah hated ironing and laundry. Matt loathed grocery shopping and errands. Right after breakfast on Saturday, he'd put a load of washing in the machine and stack some of his favorite records on the hi-fi. While the laundry went through its various cycles, he tackled the ironing, singing along happily with his favorite vocalists. Meanwhile, Sarah did the rounds of shopping and errands. She enjoyed these activities because it gave her a chance to chat with neighbors and see what was new in the shops. They both worked out successful ways to capitalize on the momentum needed for one job by relating it to something else that could be done at the same time.

## STREAMLINE YOUR HOUSEWORK—
## SCHEDULE RECURRING DEMANDS

You can streamline your housework and make it easier by following this simple principle: *Schedule recurring demands in a regular program. You will eliminate the wasted time of making decisions about when to do routine jobs.*

Decide which household chores are recurring demands. Make each one part of a smooth program by assigning it a regular time. If you know you have to clean the bathrooms once a week, don't hassle yourself each week by deciding when to do it and reminding yourself repeatedly that it must be done. Give that job a regular time, and then go ahead and do it on schedule.

Martha W. has a demanding job. She decided to schedule her laundry for Wednesday morning. She awakens forty-five minutes early that day and starts her laundry before breakfast. It's completed before she leaves for work. By doing it then, she avoids the usual evening rush waiting for washers and dryers in her apartment house's laundry room. She keeps herself on schedule by building in a special reward. The early wake-up time makes it possible for her to enjoy a leisurely breakfast, something she treasures in the middle of the week.

Grouping and scheduling recurring household demands are techniques that will help you develop a successful maintenance program. However, for special projects, you need additional techniques.

### SPECIAL PROJECTS CALL FOR SPECIAL TECHNIQUES

Some special projects—shampooing the rugs, painting the kitchen, putting up storm windows—don't occur frequently enough to build into your regular program.

First decide if the project is worth your time. Some people—especially women—set unrealistically high standards for themselves in terms of housekeeping. They spend so much time waxing the floors or cleaning out the basement that they miss many lovely sunsets, visits to the park, special times with friends. Make sure your project is worthwhile. Then go ahead and do it.

Here are two ways to get going on such a project:

1. Enlist the aid of a partner. It's much easier to accomplish things when you don't have to do it alone. When someone helps you, return the favor. Trade support with someone else who wants to get a project going. You'll both get more from your time. Also, it's easier to get help on a specific project with a foreseeable cut-off date than on an open-ended maintenance program. More friends are willing to help you paint the kitchen than to come over and help you scrub the bathroom.
2. Name your project. For example, name a project to set up a home office as "home executive." When you name

a project, you gain power over it. That's why so many people resent being labeled as a certain type by others. Naming also gives the project a handle, crystallizes its essence, and helps you keep in touch with your objective. It makes it easy to refer to. The military has done this for years. Project Desk Top, Project Safe Guard— all names that helped diverse groups mobilize their energies and concentrate on one objective.

Is there a household project that's been eluding your grasp? Go ahead and give it a name. It doesn't have to be a perfect name; you can always change it if you want to. Once you've given it a name, it's easier to clarify your objective. Then you can follow that all-important timetable technique to help you accomplish your objective. (See Chapter 14.)

### PROGRAMS, PROJECTS, AND GROUPS— TIE IT ALL TOGETHER

Demands relating to shopping and housework may seem endless. You can control the amount of time you invest in them by deciding if they are ongoing programs or one-time projects. Just put these techniques to work for you.

- Learn to relax your standards if they are too unrealistic. (Do you really have to vacuum the house more than once a week? Who's going to be hurt if you choose to invest your time in something that is more rewarding in terms of your lifestyle and accomplishments?)
- Get help when it's appropriate.
- Learn to group related activities.
- Set up ongoing programs and regular schedules for recurring demands.
- Name a special project and get a partner to help wrap it up in record time.

# 24

## EXERCISE—GET YOUR PIECE OF "PIE"

There's an increasing emphasis on physical fitness in our society. Or perhaps more correctly, there's an increasing emphasis on the dangers of being physically unfit. Despite all this attention, you may find it hard to build regular exercise into your time program. There's a management technique that can help. It's as easy as "PIE"—planning, implementation, and evaluation.

### PLANNING—DON'T JUST FOLLOW THE HERD

Even if everyone in your neighborhood plays golf, you don't have to join in if you don't enjoy the game. There are many alternatives; find one that you like, that gives you a pleasurable lift, a wonderful feeling of bodily stimulation.

A forty-three-year-old housewife and mother in my neighborhood recently won first place in a cross-country bike race. She hadn't been on a bike in twenty years until she began biking four years ago.

"I never considered myself the least bit athletic," she told me. "I was really awful at sports, or thought I was. It amounted to the same thing."

Her husband bought her a bike when she complained how hard it was to control her weight, and she discovered that she loved to ride. She got into racing just for a lark and was thrilled to realize that she was really good. Winning the cross-country confirmed it.

"I'd been on literally hundreds of exercise programs during the previous twenty years, just because I thought I should exercise," she explained. "But I never found anything I enjoyed, so I'd always quit. Now it's not a question of getting myself on the bike, it's getting myself off."

The key to this woman's success is that she *enjoyed* the exercise. Don't let that old Puritan ethic intrude on your pleasure in exercise. You don't have to suffer. Find an exercise that you enjoy, that suits you and your setting.

When you are planning, choose a form of exercise that's enjoyable *and* practical. Consult your physician to learn what is practical for your age and physical condition. If you are a lighthouse keeper on a tiny island off the coast of Maine, bike riding won't be the answer. If you want to ski, remember that it's a seasonal sport.

When you're choosing an exercise, check out what you will need in terms of equipment. Will you need a special place, a partner, or initial lessons? When you plan, consider all the costs and benefits.

## PROGRAM—NOT PROJECT

To derive maximum benefits from exercise, plan it as an ongoing program. Don't think of it in terms of a one-time project. Doctors' offices are filled with people who knock themselves out playing tennis once a month, or climbing a mountain once a year. If they haven't maintained a level of fitness through regular exercise, they wind up with pains, strains, and sprains.

## IMPLEMENTATION—
### FROM DEAD START TO FULL THROTTLE

Experts say that it takes three or four weeks of almost daily exercise to reach a point where you can accurately evaluate the benefits. Give yourself the necessary time to implement your program. During this time, don't indulge in evaluation. Exercise regularly, at least four times a week for three or four weeks, then evaluate it.

## THE WAY AROUND THE ROUGH SPOTS

During implementation, add some reinforcements and rewards to help you move beyond the rough spots. Think about how good you will feel ten minutes into your morning run— when you've hit your stride and feel the cool air on your face. Motivate yourself by thinking about a pleasure point during or after your exercise session.

John T. exercises on the racketball courts of his athletic

club. One of his greatest pleasure points is the sauna he enjoys after a particularly hard game.

Another useful reward technique is to share your accomplishments with someone else. This works particularly well when you use a friend who's also involved in some kind of exercise program. You might also consider exercising with a friend, or with a group. Joining an athletic club spurs some people on, and it's well worth the cost if it works for you.

Reward yourself with the best equipment or the most flattering outfit your exercise calls for. Often, a financial investment in an exercise program ensures that you'll stick to it and follow through.

Review the three chapters on procrastination if you want more ideas. Use any of the motivation techniques that will help you keep up with your exercise program during the implementation phase.

## EVALUATION—ADDING UP THE SCORE CARD

After three or four weeks of implementation, evaluate what you are getting from the time you invest in exercising. Most people discover that they feel much more alive and energetic. They report that they accomplish more during their "time in" and derive greater satisfaction from their work. Exercise adds to their Stimulation and Excitement Quota. If you feel you aren't getting these benefits, explore other forms of exercise.

## TIME IT RIGHT—GET MAXIMUM BENEFITS

Discover the best time to do your exercising. If you enjoy early mornings, exercise before work. You may prefer to schedule it after work to help release the pressures of the day. Many people regularly schedule lunchtimes for exercise. They skip the restaurants in favor of a sandwich at their desks and three-quarters of an hour on the tennis court, or a brisk walk. The key is setting a specific timetable.

Georgia H. never pursued any exercise program long enough to get full benefits. One day a friend told her that he'd stuck to his running program for the past year because it was a marvelous way to combat feelings of stress and depression. Georgia was a television producer with a hectic schedule. She decided regular exercise might be a better alternative than aspirin, so she took the time to establish her program. It worked.

"My jogging does more than help me cope with the stress inherent in a job like mine. It gives me time to sort things out. Problems that often look overwhelming when I am lacing up my shoes have been reduced to their proper proportions by the time I'm back at my door. What's more, I feel so much more alive and optimistic when I get regular exercise. I don't know if it will help me live longer, but it sure helps me live better every day."

## THE "PIE" TECHNIQUE PAYS OFF

Use the "PIE" technique—planning, implementation, and evaluation—to help you launch and maintain a successful exercise program. Use whatever motivation techniques you need to help you follow through during your implementation period. Exercise can help you live a more healthful life. But even more important, it can help you have a fuller, happier, more joyful life. What better return on your time can you ask?

# *Step 5.*
## Put
## Your Time
## to Work

---

## On and Off
## the Job

# 25

## PAPERWORK—FEEL BURIED BY THE AVALANCHE?

$T$his is the age of the computer printout, the copying machine, and the mass mailing—the greatest avalanche of paper the world has ever seen. It's not surprising that many people feel snowed in by mountains of paperwork. But paperwork is only a means, not an end in itself. Papers should serve you—you should not become their slave. Once you take hold of this idea, you can dig out from under and free yourself to manage your paperwork with the minimum of effort.

### QUICK QUIZ ON PAPERWORK

|  | Yes | No |
|---|---|---|
| 1. Do you believe that effectiveness equals a neat desk? | ___ | ___ |
| 2. Do you put papers in temporary parking places? | ___ | ___ |
| 3. Are you on an unusually large number of mailing lists? | ___ | ___ |
| 4. Do we keep "just in case" papers? | ___ | ___ |
| 5. Do you frequently handle papers two to three times before taking action? | ___ | ___ |
| 6. Do you try to read all the background information material rather than summaries or status reports? | ___ | ___ |
| 7. Do you always respond to letters by writing rather than sometimes calling or going in person? | ___ | ___ |

8. Do you generate a lot of attention or conversation by neglecting or mishandling your paperwork?          _____  _____

9. Do you frequently sift through stacks of paper searching for something?          _____  _____

If you answered "No" to all nine questions, you are handling your paperwork well. Any "Yes" answers indicate some problems. This chapter will show you how to use the techniques you've learned in previous chapters to clean up your paperwork problems.

## WHAT'S HIDING IN THOSE PILES OF PAPER?

Sometimes, psychological problems can generate those piles of paperwork. Unknowingly, some people use paperwork to create a disorganized impression because they actually fear success. If they looked more competent, they might get a promotion. Other people use paperwork as an excuse to avoid intimacy because they fear the feeling of closeness. Some people immerse themselves in paperwork to forestall enjoyment (that old Puritan ethic again!). They are afraid of feeling "too good"—they feel they can't enjoy themselves until they catch up on all that correspondence or finish all their reading. And that old enemy, inappropriate guilt, may crop up to aggravate the situation further.

Malcolm M. was an executive earning over $125,000 a year. But he constantly hassled himself about his paperwork problems although he knew his employers considered him a valuable asset. His bonuses consistently ran high. His boss gave him opportunities to present ideas to decisionmaking groups like the board of directors. All the signs of success were there, but they didn't alleviate his feelings of guilt about those piles of papers stacked on his desk, credenza, coffee table, window sills, and corners.

After one of my presentations, Malcolm sat down and did some more thinking about his guilt feelings. He used the techniques we discussed in Chapter 5, and was amazed at the simplicity of the solution once he concentrated on his feelings, not the paperwork itself.

"When I examined why I felt guilty, I realized that I didn't believe I deserved all my success. The paperwork didn't affect my ability to do the job in any way. I suddenly realized that the purpose of my job wasn't to have an empty 'in' basket and no papers. I was being paid for the results my department produced, not my housekeeping ability. Until I dug down to those guilt feelings, I just hadn't put it together."

This man is not alone in his struggle with nagging and destructive symptoms of inappropriate guilt about paperwork. To find out if you are subjecting yourself to inappropriate guilt feelings, ask yourself, "What contribution would I make to my own objectives and the organization's if I didn't have any paperwork problems?" If your answer is "Very little," or even "Nothing at all," your guilt feelings are out of date.

Try to uncover the psychological payoffs. You may be getting a lot of attention from your paperwork problems. Check it out—consider these questions:

- How much time do you spend talking about paperwork problems?
- Do you complain continuously about the clutter on your desk?
- Do co-workers constantly joke about your papers?

Unconsciously, you may be using your paperwork problems to get necessary stimulation from negative comments and complaints. Paperwork problems may be a replay of the same old song and dance.

Bruce B.'s secretary nagged him every day about the piles of paper he collected on his desk. Whenever she was in his office, she'd flick her fingers over yet another pile and shake her head. Periodically, he'd work furiously to clear his desk. Sometimes he even stuffed papers into his desk drawers just to get that clean-desk look. He'd invite his secretary in, show off his desk, and seek her approval. Ostensibly, it was just friendly kidding, but it was unproductive all along the line.

When Bruce examined his feelings about paperwork, it suddenly dawned on him that this was a replay of a childhood situation he'd forgotten. When Bruce was a boy, his mother would regularly come into his room, shake her head, and make sarcastic comments about the piles of comic books he collected. He went through the same periodic cleanup, too, trying to win her approval.

When he saw this current situation clearly, Bruce had to laugh. There he was, forty-five years old, a responsible, effective member of the executive team in a growing company.

Yet he'd gone out of his way to find someone to echo the same negative messages he'd received thirty-five years before.

What kind of contact and stimulation does a cluttered desk provide for you? Does any of it have an old, familiar ring?

## THE MYTH OF THE MESSY DESK

I have found that there is no direct correlation between neatness and productivity. Some very productive people have papers stacked all over their desks; others have absolutely none. A messy desk is only a sign of a messy desk. The real issue is accomplishing the work that's most important to you.

If you decide that you want to dig yourself out of those paper piles, remember these three keys to a workable system for dealing effectively with paperwork:

- Special Papers
- Special Place
- Special Time

## THE STARTING POINT—
## UNCOVER YOUR SPECIAL PAPERS

The first step is to identify the papers that contribute to your most important areas of responsibility—your central concerns and essentials. Classify these as *special papers*. Remember that Pareto's 20/80 rule means that only a few papers are vital. (See Chapter 12.) Find out which ones they are for you. Learn to handle them skillfully; they are the papers that count. No matter how much you do with the other papers, they will contribute little to your effectiveness or anyone else's.

Papers were a big problem for me for years. I could pick up three pieces of paper and lose two within five minutes. When I decided to change, I realized that it wasn't worthwhile to learn to handle *all* papers skillfully. I concentrated on two types that are vitally important to my effectiveness: manuscripts and speaking notes. These are the ones that really matter. I knew that if I concentrated on them, I'd achieve at least 80 percent results.

What types of papers do you encounter that contribute directly toward what you most want? Learn to handle these well. Let the others go, or have someone else take care of them. Avoid the perfection syndrome.

Choose your objectives *before* activities. Paperwork is an activity, not an objective. Decide what type of paperwork will contribute to your objective. If there is no direct contribution, weed it out if you possibly can. Focus on your special papers.

Answering the following question will help you assign accurate priority ratings: *What would happen if you threw this paper away?* If the answer is "Nothing," you know the paper is marginal or secondary.

Keep as few papers as possible. Reduce the volume of papers you receive by heading them off at the source. Don't just throw away a misdirected memo; call the person in charge of the distribution list and ask to be taken off. If you receive literature you don't want, send the company a postcard and ask to be removed from the mailing list. (This does not work for the I.R.S.) You'll save a great deal of time because you won't have to sort out junk mail or misdirected papers. If someone handles your incoming papers for you, tell that individual specifically what papers you do want to see and what should be done with them.

## "JUST IN CASE"

Whenever you are tempted to say, "I'm going to keep this just in case," sound an imaginary warning buzzer in your head. "Just in case" has piled up more desks, closets, and file cabinets than probably any other phrase. Concentrate on keeping only the essentials. "Just in case" papers can almost always be disposed of or handled by someone else.

People often save magazines "just in case." One data-processing project leader used to pile up magazines and journals in her bedroom and bathroom. Each time she looked at the pile, she felt guilty. She finally realized that the guilt was inappropriate because reading old magazines did not contribute to what was most important in her life.

Set time frames for keeping different kinds of papers. You may decide to read the table of contents of every magazine and throw them away after two months—read or unread. Decide how long you need to keep correspondence. Two years is sufficient for most people.

To avoid a backlog of "just in case" papers, get the material you need—when you need it—from sources that specialize in storing information. Let librarians collect articles and magazines. They are highly trained, and have all the necessary equipment and systems to make information retrieval and storage a full-time job.

A successful senior executive was tired of battling the stacks of paper he received. He decided he deserved to make life easier for himself.

"I no longer wade through an 'in' basket overflowing with 'for your information' material. I ask everyone who reports directly to me to provide a monthly report on their section's objectives and major accomplishments. They organize the information, summarize it, and present the results to me. Of course, if there is a major deviation in performance, I hear about it right away. The monthly reports also include their plans for next month and next quarter. I save time handling paperwork, and the regular reports make it easier for me to supervise them fairly."

## THE SOLUTION TO SEARCHING— A SPECIAL PLACE

Putting papers in temporary parking places on your desk or around your home can create a plague of problems.

If the paper has an important purpose, take the time to give it a special place. Where you put it is less important than the fact that it has a specific location. It's very frustrating to search for a paper you've put in a temporary place because you hadn't decided what to do with it. If the paper directly contributes to your central concerns and essentials, give it a permanent parking spot and put it there the minute you are not working on it. Do it now. (If you don't have paperwork problems, you can relax this rule. But if you are frustrated about paperwork use this special parking spot technique.)

## FACING UP TO IT—A SPECIAL TIME

Pick a regular time to deal with recurring paperwork. This will help you concentrate on one thing at a time and finish fully. For example, if mail is important in your job, assign a special time to deal with it every day. Be realistic. Set aside enough time to clear it up. Don't schedule appointments or other work for that time.

Choose a special time to sort through mail at home, too. A few minutes every day is generally more effective than two hours every two weeks. You can integrate the job by assigning a special place for items that don't require action. For example, if your special time to pay monthly bills is the 15th of the month, just put the bills aside in a file or drawer until then.

## GET A GOOD THING GOING

If you have trouble setting up a workable system to handle your paperwork, get help.

Observe someone in a similar situation—someone in your office, in another department within your company, a neighbor—who handles his or her paperwork well. Learn from them. If your organization has an administrative services or word-processing department, talk with them. Other good sources are company librarians and executive secretaries.

There are also records management consultants. You can get referrals to these professionals through many office supply companies and through local chapters of associations concerned with administrative management.

Whether you set up your own system or call on someone to help, remember the three key elements:

1. *Special papers*—concentrate on those papers that contribute directly to your objectives.
2. *Special place*—assign a special place for all important papers and put them there when you are not working on them.
3. *Special time*—set aside a special time to deal with recurring paperwork.

## KEEP IT GOING—
## THE DAILY SUCCESS STRATEGY

Now that you have set up the basics of your system, here are the techniques to use to keep it running smoothly.

Every day, sort all your papers into three priority piles:

I. Centrals and Essentials
II. Secondary Matters
III. Marginal Matters

Commit yourself to the ideal of "do it now." Throw away as many of the marginal matters as possible right now so you won't have to handle them again. Put the secondary matters aside in a special place. When you make accurate priority assessments, you'll be pleased at the number of papers you won't have to handle again. If someone asks for a paper that you designated as a secondary priority, reassign it. Schedule some time once a week or once a month to clean up remaining secondary or marginal matters.

## FOCUS AND FINISH

Now, take each piece of paper with a priority of I and decide:

1. What action should be taken?
2. Who should take it?
3. What the timetable should be.

If someone else should take action, pass it along immediately, marked with the date due. Jot the follow-up date in your calendar.

If you are going to take action, finish this paperwork fully right now if at all possible. Make the decision. Take action. You will reap a harvest of satisfaction.

If you must take action, but not for three weeks away, don't put that paper in a temporary parking spot on your desk. Put it in its special place and mark the action date on your calendar. Then forget about it until the time rolls around. The special papers are in their *special place,* and you are free to concentrate on other things. You won't waste time or clutter your mind by thumbing through the papers before the deadline for action. When you follow this procedure, you avoid just stirring the piles. You take action and move them along. Develop your ability to handle papers only once. Finish fully each time.

A financial executive told me that he trained himself to handle papers only once by glancing at a sign he has over his desk. It reads: "I dump, do, delegate or delay. These are my only options."

The right equipment can make a tremendous difference in mastering a paperwork problem. These devices can actually help you save time, and make a necessary job more enjoyable. A new little calculator may be the gadget that will help you keep up on your expense records. An alarm watch may tickle your competitive spirit into finishing a task ahead of schedule. Use whatever helps you.

Tape recorders are one of the best time-saving gadgets. You are free to answer correspondence and dictate memos when you are at your creative best. In fact, tape recorders can help you circumvent some kinds of paperwork altogether. I keep up with a great deal of personal correspondence by sending tapes instead of letters. Tapes can convey the warmth of your own voice, and they add inflection and emphasis. Experiment with new ways to handle correspondence.

## A KEY WORD OUTLINE
## TO SPUR PURPOSEFUL ACTION

When you have a letter in hand that needs an answer, use the following shortcut system:

First, jot down a three-minute key word outline.

1. In one sentence, spell out the aim of this communication. Be specific. It will make it easier to follow through with the most effective response. "I want to answer this letter" won't serve the purpose. Strive for specifics, such as, "Joe will approve my request to participate in the training seminar next month." "Mary will list her property with me exclusively." "Al will accept this as a complete answer and not write me again."

2. Next, jot down a few key words that relate to the aim of the communication. For example, key words relating to the training seminar might be:

- tuition is $500
- subject applies to my current work
- our busy season
- need replacement when I'm gone
- someone else in department attended; was productive.

Check the key words and cross out any that are not essential. Number the remaining ones in the order that is most persuasive.

3. Now decide if you can accomplish your objective best by (1) telephone call, (2) letter, or (3) meeting.

Finally, communicate the ideas. If a letter is the best response, write or dictate it immediately, using the information in the key word outline. If a call is best, use a key word outline to make a concise and complete call. If a meeting is best, the outline will help clarify the meeting objective. Finish fully and feel great.

For most of us, some amount of paperwork is inevitable. How we handle it is our choice. If you want to move those piles instead of just stirring them around, remember these techniques:

- Choose objectives before activities. Concentrate on papers that contribute to your central or essential priorities.
- Never keep something "just in case." Avoid a backlog by going to the appropriate source for information when you need it.
- Have a special place to park important papers. Put the papers away immediately after you're finished with them so you won't have to waste time searching at a later date.
- Commit yourself to taking decisive action on each paper. Do it now!
- Finish fully and feel great.

# 26

# INTERRUPTIONS—COPING
# WITHOUT BEING RUDE

In Chapter 10 we looked at some of the causes of interruptions that can throw your daily plans off schedule. Now let's examine one of the most common reasons—concern for other people's feelings.

Most of us are not willing to pursue our own objectives selfishly without considering other people. We don't like to tell friends or co-workers that their visits, calls, or conversation may be an unwelcome interruption at that moment. Whenever I speak about time, this concern is always on the tip of someone's tongue: "But I don't want to hurt their feelings." "I wouldn't have any friends." "You can't say that to the people I'm with. They just wouldn't understand." These are all valid concerns; they are based on our regard for other people. Unfortunately, these concerns often backfire.

An enthusiastic sailor and one-eighth owner of a Columbia 36 sailboat told me about her visit to a colleague's office to complete some business. Afterward, she slipped into a glowing account of last weekend's sail. As she went on about her success with a new spinnaker, the time sped by. When she later learned that her colleague was being pressured to meet an important deadline while she was chattering away, she said, "I felt so foolish. I wish he had told me."

## INCONSIDERATE OR JUST UNAWARE?

I believe that most people want to help you with your time. They want to respect it, but they may stay too long, talk at the wrong time, or interrupt you when you are concentrating on a rush project. They don't do it deliberately. They get carried away by their own enthusiasm, or their lack of knowledge about the pressures you are facing.

After an enjoyable breakfast with a friend at a neighborhood restaurant, I stopped by her house to admire a massive oak chest that she had refinished. As I continued to chat, she said something that I really appreciated.

"Dru, I'm feeling pressured about the shopping I need to do for the family today. I had a lovely breakfast with you, and now I need to be moving on to my chores." Her directness adds pleasure to my time with her. I have the comfort of knowing that when we're together, it's because she wants to be there. I'm never on edge wondering if I've called at an inconvenient time, or overstayed my welcome.

One man endeared himself to a special single lady in his life by checking whenever he called her at home, "Am I calling at a good time for you?" She said that his thoughtfulness in asking that question saved her several embarrassing moments and heightened her opinion of him.

## THE DIRECT APPROACH—TELL IT LIKE IT IS

Take the time to let others know *directly* the pressures you're under and the deadlines you face. Learn to do it with tact and skill. Others do appreciate us more when we maintain a healthy amount of concern about feelings, and at the same time mix in thoughtful communication skills.

Some people don't believe this. They share the sentiment expressed by a young physician: "I shouldn't have to tell colleagues when I'm busy. They should know I don't have time to talk when I keep my pen in hand, poised over a stack of papers." That's not direct enough. It's not efficient and thoughtful.

If a friend is rhapsodizing about her new house, and you appear distant or indifferent because you're worrying about leaving for an appointment that you haven't mentioned, she's likely to start questioning your friendship. You could save hours of explanation and apology by telling her immediately that you're rushed and that you'd like to talk about her new house as soon as you get back. Then she knows that you're interested in what she has to say, and won't have reason to misunderstand your preoccupation.

## ADD A DASH OF DIPLOMACY

There are several direct and courteous ways to let others know that you don't have time to chat, without running the risk of hurt feelings.

You might say, "Your weekend trip to Miami sounds great. It's certainly more appealing than the project I'm working on right now."

Or, "I'm pleased about your new marketing plan. Right now I'm just so distracted by the noon deadline that's coming up that I'm not concentrating on you as much as I'd like to."

One woman found that reaching out to touch a talkative friend lightly on the arm was a tactful way to get him to pause in the conversation. Then she could explain that she was busy and would be able to talk with him later.

What about the people who take up your time on the phone? Remember, they can't see that you are surrounded by anxious people, and in imminent danger of being crushed by a tottering stack in your "in" basket. It's only courteous to let them know the pressure you're under at the moment.

You might say, "I'm glad you called, Jim. Catching up on the news with you is always a lift. If I had my way, I'd put my feet up and talk with you and forget this stack of work. But I think I had better keep plowing through it. I'm glad you called and that we had a minute to touch base."

## "BUT IT'S THE BOSS!"

If you are interrupted by your boss, you have an opportunity to use even more skill since it's a situation that's costly to ignore. First, ask yourself, "Is listening to my boss part of my job?" If your boss is someone who analyzes and puts together ideas by talking out loud, listening may be part of your job. On the other hand, your boss may not know your pressures and concerns.

Deborah T. solved this situation by learning to say, "I'm excited about what we can do with this new account [or whatever subject the boss is talking about]. I'm assuming that your interest means our conversation now is more important than the cost figures I have to put together for the Cline account." In this way she verified that she was interested in what her boss was saying, and confirmed that the conversation had a higher priority than the cost figures.

By this time you may be saying, "You don't know my boss." You're right. You do need to examine your situation and the personalities involved, then decide what will work best for you. There are no pat answers when you're dealing with people.

Even the most tactful comment will not work if your voice tone, facial gestures, and posture do not convey respect and care. You probably know someone who uses all the right phrases, but really believes that people are shabby excuses for using up oxygen. Skillful phrases *add* to respect; they do not substitute for it.

## RESPECT YOUR OWN TIME

Concern for others can certainly complicate time. Learn to use the techniques in this chapter to balance this concern with the respect your own time deserves. Tell people directly what your time frame is; ask what pressures they are facing. As you build and practice these skills, you'll have more time to achieve your objectives and help those around you to achieve theirs. You will be showing concern for others in new ways.

Look continually for new ways to help your friends, family, and work associates give your time the respect it deserves. Allow time to be a rich resource for *all* of us to enjoy.

# 27

# THE TELEPHONE—
# TOOL OR TYRANT

When Alexander Graham Bell invented the telephone in 1876, he thought he'd given the world a valuable tool. Little did he know that one day many people would come to regard his marvelous invention as nothing short of a tyrant. The telephone intrudes on privacy, interrupts work, ruins repose. People often tell me that they could manage their time wonderfully well if it weren't for the telephone.

If you consistently mismanage your telephone time, there's no doubt that it can become a tyrant. But used to your advantage, it is a wonderfully helpful tool. It's up to you.

## WHAT'S EATING UP YOUR TELEPHONE TIME?

If you feel your time is being eaten up by the telephone, first learn where your time is going.

Ask yourself these questions about each call you make or receive during the next five days. Write your answers in your time management notebook:

1. With whom did you talk?
2. Who initiated the call?
3. What was covered?
4. What was achieved?

Making these notes can lead to some valuable insights. Most people discover that rarely *everyone* they know wastes time on the telephone. Typically, it's a very small group of people. Sometimes, people discover that *they themselves* initiate the time-wasting calls.

Paul B. handled the financial records for a huge chain of sporting good stores. He realized that although he complained about his time on the phone, he really liked it. "Most of my work is very isolated. I don't talk to many people during the day. Consequently, when I get tired working only with figures, I start finding telephone calls I just have to make."

Know what you get from your telephone time; you may discover that phone "interruptions" are really sources of excitement and stimulation. Before you give up the phone calls, substitute something more positive. Or decide to accept your need for stimulation and work out ways to make your phone calls more productive and satisfying.

Next, come to grips with the question, What was covered? When you're jotting down your notes, be aware of how much time was spent talking about the weather, or in casual conversation.

What you achieved during the telephone conversation is the next consideration. "Returning a call" is not an achievement; it's an activity. You may find that your time is wasted because people call you without leaving a complete message. When you call back, you don't know the objective of the call. Keeping track of what was achieved gives you an easier way of determining necessary changes.

## SPEAK RIGHT UP—SAY WHAT YOU WANT

Before you place a telephone call, decide specifically what you want to accomplish. Jot down two or three items on your calendar or note pad and then check them off as you cover them during the call. If it's a personal call, reaffirm your objective to "make contact." Knowing what you want to accomplish lets you know when you're through.

Bernie L. was the manager for new market development for a middle-sized manufacturing company with plants scattered around the country. He traveled regularly one week out of every month. While on the road, he'd run up enormous telephone bills calling home. Bernie had to define what he wanted to accomplish with these calls after his boss started questioning that item on his expense account. He had to admit that he and his family mostly talked about the weather.

When he sat down and thought about it, Bernie realized that he made those calls because he wanted to establish contact with his wife and children. He wanted to know that they were all right. He wanted to feel that they missed him and appreciated what he was doing for them. So he gathered the family together before his next trip and told them directly just what he wanted to accomplish with those nightly calls. From then on, he got what he wanted, and his family benefitted because they were helping him. Now when he calls he gives the family shorthand signal, "I've called for a weather report." They know he wants to hear the details of their day, and be reassured that they love him and will be happy to have him home again. Bernie gets what he wants and cuts down on phone bills.

## THE SAME OLD NUMBERS

Your notes can also help you spot recurring problems. For instance, do many of your phone calls result from your inability to meet deadlines? Do your co-workers and supervisors call constantly for explanations of delays? Do you have to make a lot of calls to get extensions on the deadline, or explain why the expected report won't be ready until next Tuesday? In such a case, the phone is not the problem; your difficulty in meeting deadlines is.

Do you have friends or relatives who constantly call for no specific reason, engaging you in time-consuming chats about nothing important? Maybe they are feeling neglected. They may want to be reassured that you still value them. You might eliminate those irritating interruptions by setting aside a few minutes at regular intervals to call them and initiate a chat. Help satisfy their needs but do it at a time that's best for you.

## MAKE THE BEST CONNECTION—
## BE CONSIDERATE

Be considerate of others when you call them. It only takes a couple of seconds to ask, "Is this a convenient time for you to talk?" Those few seconds can make such a difference for you. If it is not convenient for the other person, you won't be getting his or her full attention. Work out a phrase that fits your time management style. Use it when you call others. It may encourage them to be more considerate of your time.

When people phone you, it's also important to be considerate. Let them know if you are under pressures rather than merely giving them your divided attention. Since this is a difficult area for many people, have several expressions ready that you can use if this occurs. For example:

"I have a rush project on my desk right now and I would like to call you back this afternoon. Will that work for you?"

"I'm enjoying our conversation, but I have some urgent deadlines on my mind. May I call you back tomorrow?"
"I have company right now. When may I call you back tomorrow?"

If you let people rattle on when it's not convenient, you're not really doing them a favor or being polite. If you allow them to impose on your time *before* you tell them it's not convenient to talk, they are going to feel embarrassed and annoyed. So do everyone a favor. Learn to say, "May I call you back later?" in whatever manner best suits your style and your situation.

## GET FAST RESULTS—
## CONTROL THE CONVERSATION

Start your conversation quickly and skillfully. Your voice tone can carry warmth and respect. Five minutes of conversation about the football game or some other routine topic is not a necessary warm-up. Most people appreciate it when you take the time to think out what you want to accomplish with a phone call, and get to the point right away. It saves their time as well as yours. Handled courteously and in a friendly tone, it's usually a most welcome manner of conducting business by telephone.

## HOW TO SAY GOODBYE AND HANG UP

In a business setting particularly, it is appropriate for either person to signal the close of the call when business is completed. Talking about the call in the past tense is an effective way to close the conversation gently.

- "That sounds like we've wrapped up most of the issues. Is there anything else we need to talk about before we close the call?"
- "I'm glad you called. It has been good checking over these items before the meeting."
- "I'm glad we've had this opportunity to bring each other up to date. It's been good talking with you."

## THE JOY OF UNPLUGGING

Unplugging the phone can be a physical action or a state of

mind. One successful author starts her day with meditation that is never interrupted by a jangling phone because she actually unplugs the telephone first. Others can concentrate so fully that they can mentally unplug and ignore the sounds of the phone.

You may tell people, "My phone is unplugged until noon," to let them know that you prefer taking calls during the afternoon. It doesn't necessarily have to be unplugged. If you can't unplug the telephone (perhaps you have small children in school and need to be available for any calls), invest in a recording device. Even forty-five minutes or an hour of unterrupted time can be useful, and you won't miss any important calls.

If you don't want to make such an investment, you can find ways to "unplug" your phone when you want to have free time. One young man who was establishing himself as a freelance writer couldn't afford to miss any calls from his agent, but he also needed to concentrate on his work without interruption. He worked out a system whereby he would call his agent's office at regular times during the day for messages. He never missed hearing about an assignment, and he never had to interrupt his flow of thought to answer the phone.

Rebecca S. was a young mother who finally got the last of her four children into kindergarten. She rewarded herself for all those years of constant child care with free mornings for painting, a lifelong passion of hers. In case of an emergency, she gave the school office a code to use between nine and noon: ring twice, hang up, and dial again. She gave the same signal to her husband, her mother, her children, and a neighbor. This covered all possible contingencies and left her free to ignore the phone at other times.

## PEOPLE COME FIRST

Stay in touch with the reality that the telephone is only a tool. By giving it power over your time, *you* are the one who makes it a tyrant. No matter how important the phone may seem, remember that people come first. Use it skillfully and it will enhance your time and your life.

- Tell people what you want directly.
- Be considerate—make the best connection.
- Take hold of the conversation at the start.
- Develop tact and skill in closing a call.

# 28

## ARE YOU A WORKAHOLIC?

The label "workaholic" is tossed around rather carelessly today, although the definition of "workaholic" is certainly not exact. I've worked with and studied hundreds of people who put in many hours every week, but they are not workaholics. They are highly productive and derive a great deal of satisfaction from their jobs. They are able to measure their work time in terms of steady movement toward accomplishing objectives that are important to them. Most significant of all, they quickly relax and forget their work completely when they want to. They have also developed the ability to pick up and get going again rapidly. Like a light switch, they are "on" or "off" fully, with little halfway time in between.

### ONLY YOU CAN DECIDE

Knowing how many hours you work a week is important, but that alone will not tell you if you are a workaholic. The ten questions below can help you decide if your work is in a healthy balance with your total time investment. Since so many people receive unhealthy, negative stimulation and recognition from the number of hours they work, go through this list alone. Don't discuss it with your partner or co-workers right now. Consider each question carefully, and be honest with yourself.

### TEN KEY QUESTIONS

|  | Yes | No |
|---|---|---|
| 1. Do you have a difficult time sitting still and doing nothing? | ____ | ____ |
| 2. Do you take work along with you to social or pleasurable events? | ____ | ____ |
| 3. Do you find it difficult to relax without | | |

the use of alcohol or some other sub-
stance?    ____  ____

4. Do you frequently think about work during times of relaxation or sexual ecstasy? ____  ____

5. Do you sometimes enjoy having others
know that you work long hours?    ____  ____

6. Do you have trouble really letting go
and allowing yourself to have fun?    ____  ____

7. When you take a day off or go on vacation, do you leave a telephone number
where you can be reached? If someone
from work calls you, do you feel a certain sense of pleasure and importance?    ____  ____

8. When you actually add up the number
of hours a week you worked during the
last four weeks, do you wish you could
cut down that number?    ____  ____

9. Have you gone three or more years
without taking at least a two-week vacation without work?    ____  ____

10. Are your time investments out of balance when you consider them in terms
of work, play, and love?    ____  ____

Although there are no absolute answers, consider making
some changes if you marked more than three Yeses. Only
you can define the role that work has in your life. Take some
time to think it through. Recognizing that you are a workaholic isn't easy to face, but it is always better to know the
facts than to coast along blindly, merely hoping that things
will work themselves out.

A cartoon I saw recently shows two men talking on a
street corner. The thought-provoking caption read: "I owe all
my success to my family. I didn't want to go home, so I
worked late every night." Often the real stimulus for extra

hours at work isn't the job itself, but what we would be doing if we weren't working.

The cartoon's logic doesn't hold up, however. When avoidance is the real motivation, an individual is more likely to function in a compulsive mode. (See Chapter 8.) People playing a compulsive Try Hard role may consistently spend an extra three or four hours on the job but accomplish much less than they would if they invested fewer hours and operated from choice.

If you are concerned about the amount of time you work, imagine what you would be doing if you didn't work at all. If you had an independent income, what would you be doing with your time? Would you enjoy whatever activity you chose, and would you know *how* to do it? If you grew up with a group of people who worked constantly, you may not know how to relax and have fun. Now ask yourself if you feel that you deserve your imaginary choice.

Motivation that stems from avoidance is not a good idea in any time investment, and it's potentially dangerous in terms of work.

A parent may get immersed in long hours on the job to avoid facing his or her teenager's drug problem.

A partner in a decaying relationship may flee from frank discussion of the problem by taking on an inhuman workload.

An individual may hide from the reality of a barren personal life by burying fears and feelings under tons of extra work.

A successful executive may increase her standards of job performance to avoid the realization that she already has far exceeded her parents' expectations for her. She may be reacting to a childhood fear that if she is more successful than her parents, they won't love her.

## ARE LONG HOURS
## THE PRICE OF SUCCESS?

Many of the most effective and highly paid top executives I know do not work more than forty hours a week. The sixty- or seventy-hour work week does not 'come with the territory of success. Yet many people use success to justify spending most of their evenings in work- or job-related entertaining. Some subtle assumptions prop up this behavior. Sometimes it is a feeling that you have to pay for your success by sacrificing some part of your personal life. This is another variation of an inability to enjoy success fully.

Another stimulus for some people who work long hours is the naked fact that their work may be more interesting than anything or anyone else in their lives. They enjoy what happens at work more than what happens at home. I'm not criticizing this. If that's your situation, it's healthier to face it squarely because you can always deal with life and your time more effectively when you understand your motivations accurately.

The fear of enjoyment runs so deep in many people that they compulsively occupy themselves with work and more work to prevent any rays of enjoyment from streaming into their lives. Even though this fear of feeling good isn't rational, it's very common.

Another aspect of the fear of enjoyment is the old myth that if you hold yourself back from enjoyment, you can somehow help someone else. You don't need to fear pleasure or enjoyment because it might diminish the opportunity for others to enjoy themselves. These ideas are not accurate. Replace them with more productive strategies. It's all right for you to be as successful and important as you want to be.

## SAVE TIME BY SAVORING SUCCESS

If an objective that you struggled to achieve has an empty ring once you reach it, you may need to learn how to enjoy your successes more fully. Allow yourself the full range of sensations and delights available when you accomplish something important to you. You'll get more from your time if you savor your success. It will help pull you off that tiring workaholic treadmill of "never enough."

## THE SELF-EMPLOYED WORKAHOLIC

Not all workaholics are in paid employment. Owners of small businesses and full-time homemakers have the toughest problem knowing how much is enough. There's always something else to be done and no boss to say, "That's enough. Punch the time clock and go home." That's why it's so important to use the techniques we've discussed for setting objectives, doing essentials first, finishing fully, knowing what tasks count most. They can help the homemaker or small business owner escape the clutches of the workaholic syndrome. They also open doors to personal freedom and quality time that are so vitally necessary, especially for those carrying the heavy responsibilities of full-time homemaking.

## DO THE BOOKS BALANCE?

If you suspect that you are a workaholic, the first step I recommend is to make sure that you aren't using work as a shield to avoid something. Then, set up a healthy mixture of time invested in work, play, and love. No one else can define exactly what the right balance is for you, so decide for yourself what you want more or less of.

Balance will not automatically drift into your life, but you can create it by managing your time creatively and consistently every day. Take action every day to move you closer to the mixture you want.

Justice Oliver Wendell Holmes, a hard worker and outstanding achiever, indicated the importance of constant creativity in managing your life when he said, "Life is painting a picture, not doing a sum." You *deserve* free time and quality relationships and you *need* them. A healthy amount of time for play boosts your ability to tackle even the biggest workload with zest. And have you noticed how much energy you have when you are in love?

## DOING AND BEING—A VITAL DISTINCTION

Our capacity for accomplishments, recreation, and relationships grows from a strong sense of our personal value, our being. No amount of work and no accomplishment can confirm or challenge our being, because being does not depend on doing. Doing can lead to satisfaction and the sense of accomplishment, but it will never substitute for the realization of your own personal worth. Affirm your value as a multifaceted individual. Enjoy a rich variety of time investments. Open yourself to the joys of this moment whether they are in recreation, relationships, or work accomplishments.

# 29

# FIVE STEPS
# TO FRUSTRATION-FREE
# TIME WITH YOUR BOSS

---

**W**herever and whenever I make presentations to various organizations, I run into complaints about "the boss." People say they can't ever get enough time with the boss. There are always interruptions, or the boss doesn't listen, or the boss doesn't respond in desired ways.

In short, thousands of people are wasting time feeling frustrated because they aren't getting what they want from the boss. If that's how you feel, there are five steps that you can take to solve the problem.

## STEP 1:
### DISCOVER ANY UNSATISFIED WANTS

Feelings of frustration about the boss may spring up because your needs have changed. When you first began your current job, you may only have been able to handle the responsibilities then assigned. Now, you may be eager to take on new responsibilities, receive a promotion, or expand your job description. Make sure you're up to date on unsatisfied wants.

Many people turn to their bosses for things they wanted and did not get enough of from their parents. For example, Andrew L. constantly complained that his boss didn't appreciate him. It turned out that "appreciate" in Andrew's terms meant the total love and acceptance children want and deserve from their parents. This rarely comes from a boss. If you know you wanted to be accepted more fully by your parents when you were a child, realize that you may want an unrealistic amount of approval from your boss. Unconditional acceptance as a human being adds stability and richness to each day, and certainly should be sought from your family and the other special people in your life. Unfortunately, too many people seek it from their boss.

People who confuse the role of their families and their organizations waste time on the job. I've run into dozens of executives who want their management teams to love them and their families to work for them. Regardless of how much time they invest in their team, they rarely get love and total acceptance from their subordinates. This is a futile time investment.

Learn to assess what you want from your boss objectively. Is it realistic or unrealistic, old or current?

## STEP 2: KNOW WHAT YOU WANT MOST FROM THE BOSS

We all have a collection of wants and expectations relating to the boss. The most time-effective strategy is to put them in priority order and concentrate on what we want *most*.

We all want money, and most of us want more of it. But don't assume that money is always going to be at the top of your list of priorities. Perhaps you are more interested in variety in work assignments, more opportunity for creativity, more verbal feedback from the boss on the value of your work, or forty-five minutes of your boss's undivided attention to talk about an important project.

Although you can't always get what you want, it will save time to know what that is. This knowledge frees you to act if you choose; to decide if your needs are realistic and appropriate. Take the time to discover what you want most from your boss right now. Consider actions, work assignments, responses—even how you want your boss to feel about you. You can't *make* people feel anything, but you *can* know what you want.

If you decide to act, consider the best way to get what you want. Perhaps you want your boss to feel confident that you are doing a good job. The fastest way to do that might be to wrap up the assignment you're working on and send your boss a memo summarizing the results of the project. If you want forty-five minutes of your boss's time to discuss a project you are now working on, you could request an appointment. For example, you might say, "I'd like forty-five minutes of your time one day this week to bring you up to date on the Bemis case, and get your advice on which of two possible alternatives would accomplish most in terms of the company's overall objectives."

## *STEP 3:* KNOW WHAT YOUR BOSS WANTS FROM YOU

When you don't know what your boss wants from you, you are at a serious disadvantage. You may run the risk of being fired, losing a promotion, missing out on a raise. No matter how "secure" your job may be on paper, if you don't know what your boss wants from you, you can waste a lot of time.

Having this knowledge doesn't mean that you have to fulfill all your boss's needs. It does mean that you have the freedom to act to your best advantage; to operate from a position of reality rather than fantasy.

Before you begin gathering up-to-date information on what your boss wants from you, learn to accept what may be a crushing blow—your boss probably doesn't think about you as much as you think about your boss. Most bosses have enough to do without preoccupying themselves with individual subordinates. So exercise tact in getting the information you need directly from your boss. Select a time when your boss is least likely to be pressured by deadlines and commitments. Make a scheduled appointment. This will let your boss know that you want feedback seriously. Use any variation of the wording below that suits your own style.

"We have worked together for several years. I want to make sure that I'm doing the kind of job you most want and the organization needs. When would it be convenient for us to spend thirty minutes of uninterrupted time together to discuss this?"

During your time together, don't talk about whether your boss likes you. Talk about what you produce. Use questions to get a clear picture of your boss's needs. Use the "want more of, want less of" approach. "For me to do an even better job, what do I need to do more of? Less of?" The "less of" question often uncovers negative information that otherwise would remain undisclosed. People's careers can be stifled and their effectiveness can be limited because they don't discover negative information in time.

Make sure the feedback is specific enough to be useful. For example, if your boss wants you to communicate better, explore that further. Your tone is very important at this stage; don't sound defensive. You could say:

"I'm glad you mentioned a developmental area that I can improve. When you say 'communicate better,' I want to make sure I understand exactly what you mean. Can you give me an example of what I will be doing when I communicate better? Will it be in terms of written communication, or meetings, or some other area?"

Don't assume you understand what the boss wants until you have a specific example or guideline. If you were to ask fifteen people to think of a car, each would think of a specific car. Unless you gave an example, a 1973 yellow Buick Century, it's unlikely any of the fifteen would think of that particular car.

## STEP 4: LEARN WHAT YOUR BOSS WANTS

In the same way that we often project what we wanted from our parents onto our boss, we also project our own motivations onto the boss. A classic example is the hard-driving subordinate who wants to move up, and the boss who is settled and content with the status quo. Not all bosses are ambitious. Some are treading water.

Don't project your own motivations onto your boss. Instead, speculate on the kinds of pressures, fears, and hopes he or she might feel. You'll never know these exactly, but you can make some informal guesses. These guesses always take second place to anything your boss communicates directly through conversation or behavior, but they will help you track what your boss wants for himself or herself.

Understand that your boss may have tremendous pressures, and may be worrying about losing his or her own job, not about promoting you. You can always make better decisions and be more effective when you face life directly and understand the realities of the situation.

## STEP 5:
## TREAT YOUR BOSS LIKE A CUSTOMER

Treat your boss like a valued customer. That's the way a wise and experienced manufacturer's representative summed it up for me.

Years ago, Grant V. learned that in order to get the commitment he wanted from his boss, he had to treat his boss with the same skill and consideration he showed his best customers. "I remind myself continually that my boss could change suppliers," Grant said. "Keeping this in mind has made it possible for me to work with him successfully. Plus, when I think of my boss as a customer, I don't mind calling on my skills. It becomes another marketing or selling situation. Getting the commitment I want from the boss becomes the sales goal."

Help your boss get what he or she wants. Know what you are offering the boss, what your product is. Fundamentally, that's why you are on the payroll.

When you want your boss to do something that benefits you, take time to figure out what's in it for the boss. Don't expect twenty-four-hour-a-day altruism from your boss. That isn't realistic. Whenever you want some time with the boss, ask yourself, "How will the boss benefit by giving me this time?" Your objective is to make the boss eager to spend time with you, and the best way to achieve that is to make the time beneficial for your boss as well.

## MARKETING TO THE BOSS

As you develop this marketing approach, consider the best way to present your product. Communicate in the ways and methods that your boss favors. Some of us prefer to see things in written form; others like to hear about it first hand. If you go in to talk things over with the boss, and he concludes the session with a request for a memo on the situation, it's evident the boss prefers the written word to the spoken word. Don't waste time using the wrong means of communication.

## UPDATE YOUR MARKETING PROGRAM

- Use the five steps in this chapter to develop an effective time program with your boss.
- Keep your program up to date by doing a marketing study and product evaluation every six months; include a scheduled meeting with your boss to determine if his or her wants have changed.
- Update your own wants.
- Remember that optimizing your time with the boss is an ongoing process.

# 30

## MAKE YOUR MEETING
## TIME COUNT

Unstructured, time-consuming meetings are a major complaint across the country. The indictment falls not only on formal meetings but on those corridor conferences that spontaneously develop when someone grabs you and says, "Do you have a minute?" Twenty minutes later, you're still talking and nothing has been resolved.

### A MEETING BILL OF RIGHTS

Since meetings involve other people, a team approach is necessary if leaders and participants alike are going to get the most from their time. A Meeting Bill of Rights gives everyone involved the right to know *in advance:*

1. the meeting objective
2. what question the meeting should answer
3. what each participant is expected to contribute
4. what time the meeting will be over.

When you are sending out a notice for a meeting, make sure it covers the four points of the Meeting Bill of Rights. It's a fast way to guarantee that your meeting time will count. If you are invited to a meeting and this information isn't given in advance, ask.

### CLARIFY OBJECTIVES IN ADVANCE

Knowing the objective before the meeting provides a focus for the meeting, and a yardstick by which to measure accomplishments.

Paula R. used this technique to chop six hours from her weekly schedule. As director of parks and recreation for a large county, she was continually involved in drawn-out meetings that failed to accomplish much of anything. Rather than

198

continue complaining, she decided what she wanted and tackled the problem directly. At the start of every meeting, she expressed her understanding of the purpose and checked others' objectives. After doing this at each meeting for just two weeks, she discovered that she had "trained" both her subordinates and her boss. They had all become accustomed to clarifying meeting objectives, and were no longer sidetracked by the free-floating, rambling discussions that formerly wasted so much group time.

Paula went a step further and taught her secretary these skills. When someone schedules an appointment with Paula, her secretary courteously asks, "I want to have everything ready for your appointment. The director said it will help if I can tell her what you'd like to accomplish during your meeting."

At first, Paula was concerned that she might miss out on valuable grapevine information, but that wasn't the case. Interesting meeting objectives began to show up on her calendar: "Fifteen minutes to give you the scuttlebutt on last night's commission meeting"; "Ten minutes to tell you about the project I completed ahead of schedule."

This technique can be useful even in a corridor conference. When someone stops us for an off-the-cuff meeting, we often waste time assuming we know what they walk to talk about. But often, people who present a problem aren't looking for a solution from you. Sometimes, they just want sympathy, or appreciation for working independently.

The next time Joe stops you to talk about accounts receivable, immediately let him know that you want to make sure you understand what he wants from you. Use questions to save time for both of you. "What can I do for you?" "What do you need from me that will help you solve that problem?" "What is it that you want from me?" Make sure that your tone of voice doesn't convey anger or impatience.

## CLUE THEM WITH QUESTIONS

Advance notice of the specific questions to be asked during a meeting can save more time than a list of topics. For example, the topic "Safety" doesn't lend itself to adequate preparation as much as the question, "How can we reduce at least two lost-time accidents in each division?"

## SPECIFY WHAT'S EXPECTED

If group participation is necessary, let people know what is required of them before the meeting. If your meeting is designed to develop regional sales strategies for the next quarter, you will need individual reports from six salespeople who service different territories. State the meeting objective and list the questions that will be asked. Then point out that you need a specific report from each salesperson to help clarify the conditions on which regional forecasts will be made.

When you clarify objectives and give advance notice on questions and specific contributions, everyone is better prepared to concentrate. Your meetings will be more productive.

## STATE THE CLOSING TIME

Be specific about the meeting's time limit and stick to the specified closing time. People accomplish much more when there is a firm closing time for a meeting. This is a proven psychological principle that works in therapy as well as in the office.

Bob and Mary McClure Goulding, West Coast psychologists, implement this technique in group therapy sessions. They set a firm guideline of twenty minutes for each individual, and they begin and close group sessions on time. Once clients recognize that twenty-minute time frame, it's remarkable how much they accomplish. The most significant part of most therapy sessions is the final ten minutes, regardless of the total length of the session. We accomplish more when we have a closing time.

If people frequently run overtime, schedule your closing to coincide with lunch or the end of the day. However, the closing time should not be a rigid point if business is completed quickly. If you meet the objectives earlier, close the meeting. It's an extra incentive to good time use.

## WRAP IT UP NEATLY

Get into the habit of ending meetings with a summary of what has been accomplished and assigned. A summation can be as brief as, "To wrap up our meeting, here's what I think we've pulled together. We've decided not to pursue the Jones contract until next quarter. Joe will take responsibility for monitoring the program until we follow through in June. Jane will get the figures we need for the Carter project and present them at the meeting on March 5. Have I missed any other accomplishments or assignments?" It's a useful technique even in a corridor conference. Wrap up decisions and accomplishments by saying, "Bill, will you let me know how this works out by Friday?" "Chris, I'll stop by your office this afternoon so we can have an uninterrupted fifteen minutes of talk."

## CASH IN ON ACCRUED BENEFITS EVERY TIME

Collecting accrued benefits is a technique that provides a bonus when you solve any time problem, and the technique is particularly helpful for meetings. Solve each problem with the larger picture in mind. The solution itself offers an immediate benefit, and you can use it in another way to collect further benefits. It's the "two-for-the-price-of-one" time management technique. Here's an example of how it works:

John H. noticed that a number of the account executives he supervised asked for his help to solve new and complicated tax shelter problems. He realized that he could get an even better return on his time investment by following these steps:

1. Manager helps account executive define the problem.
2. Account executive prepares recommended solution.
3. Manager reviews solution with account executive and they make needed modifications together.
4. Account executive uses the solution with client. (This is the one-time benefit.)
5. Account executive then presents the case and solution to entire staff during training meeting. The account executive receives public acknowledgment for successful handling of the situation. Other staff members learn new solutions. The manager saves more time because the staff can work independently more often. (These are the accrued benefits.)

A meeting planner for a large corporation saved dozens of hours using the accrued benefit technique. Whenever there was a problem in a meeting, she tracked down the source, solved it on the spot, and made a note of it. Later she incorporated that note into her master checklist for meetings.

"When the overhead projector bulb went out in a half-hour meeting I had planned, it took forty-five minutes to track down a spare bulb. I decided that 'spare bulb' was going to be part of my advance preparation checklist."

Whenever you solve a problem, consider how you can use that solution to make time in the future. Use this technique to turn persistent problems into time-saving procedures.

A newly employed financial analyst was confronted with tough questions that he just couldn't handle in the first few meetings with his boss. At the conclusion of each meeting, he wrote down the questions and researched the information he needed to answer them immediately. Then he went a step further and began analyzing the types of questions his boss asked. Before the next meeting, he went over the agenda and prepared himself to answer similar kinds of questions.

There are many other ways this technique can be useful. For example, if you have written a note to a friend and his address is missing from your address book, you might thumb through last year's Christmas cards to get the address from an envelope. That's a direct benefit. When you write it in your address book, that's the accrued benefit. It's a simple technique that can make time by preventing and preparing for problems.

*Use some extra creativity every time you solve any problem and get an accrued benefit.*

Even the Meeting Bill of Rights has accrued benefits. You'll benefit directly by saving time during meetings when you follow the four steps. And you'll collect the accrued benefits of meeting with responsible people who have developed the ability to think more creatively and effectively.

Whether it's a formal meeting or a corridor conference, your meeting time will count when you let participants know in advance:

- what the objectives are
- what questions the meeting should answer
- what is expected of them
- what the closing time is

You generate follow-through when you end each meeting with a brief summary, and you give yourself a bonus on your time investment when you collect accrued benefits.

# 31

## "YES" IS A TIME TRAP WHEN YOU WANT TO SAY "NO"

If you've had the experience of working with someone who says "Yes" to requests he or she does not fulfill, you know how much time can be wasted. Deadlines are missed, work must be reassigned, sometimes extra help must be hired to fill in at the last minute. In social situations, people accept invitations to boring parties, run errands for family and friends when they really don't have time, agree to take on volunteer duties that they can't possibly cram into their schedules.

In a host of ways, many of us allow our precious time to be eaten away by demands that we wish we could say "No" to. The trigger for this time waste comes in dozens of different ways. Do you say "Yes" for any of these reasons?

- You don't want to hurt someone's feelings.
- You don't want to explain why you want to say "No."
- You don't want to say anything that the other person might interpret as negative.
- You feel obligated to spend time with the person because you haven't seen her or him in months.
- The other person is particularly important to you.
- You would really like to oblige, but the timing is inappropriate.

Luckily, there are several proven psychological techniques that can free you from the bind of saying "Yes" when you don't want to, and help you learn how to say "No" skillfully and tactfully.

First, let's take a look at this typical family situation. It illustrates what can happen when someone learns to say "No" creatively.

### "CATCH UP ON THE CLEVELAND CROWD"

Whenever John's older brother, Bud, came to town, it was a

frustrating situation for John and his wife Mary. Bud was the move-in-and-take-over type. John would get a call at the office and hear a hearty, "Hiya, kid! We're in town again! We'll be out for dinnner around seven, okay? Got lots to tell you; good chance to get you caught up on the old crowd in Cleveland."

For years, John never had the heart to say "No." He thought that he owed it to his brother to be available; that But and Nancy would be hurt if he and Mary weren't hospitable. He and Mary would cancel their own plans and settle in for a long evening of catching up on Cleveland.

Over the years, a pattern developed. The call would come, Bud and Nancy would arrive for drinks and conversation, they would all decide where to eat, then leave for the restaurant. After dinner, they'd return to John's for what Bud liked to refer to as a "real heart to heart." This, along with several more drinks, might stretch out until after midnight. At that point John and Mary would ask Bud and Nancy to stay overnight, so more time was spent making up the guest room, getting out towels, finding pajamas, etc. Then there was a company breakfast to look forward to preparing.

## PLAN AND PREVENT

John and Mary finally decided to do something about Bud and his periodic invasions.

First they defined what they wanted: a three- or four-hour leisurely dinner with relatives when they were in town. Then they defined what they didn't want: last-minute self-invitations that meant they had to rearrange their own plans at a moment's notice. With this in mind, John sat down and wrote the following note to his brother:

Dear Bud,
Great to see you last week, and fine to hear how things are going in Cleveland. We're both looking forward to your next visit. To make sure we don't have plans that will interfere without getting together, will you give us a call a couple of weeks in advance? That way, we can make all the arrangements and won't have to cut into the conversation to take care of details while you're here.

Some months later, Bud roared into town in his usual fashion, called to surprise John, and ran head on into a new John. John and Mary had foreseen that Bud might "forget" to call ahead, so they'd practiced for just such an encounter.

In a firm but friendly manner, John explained that they had some previous commitments that would make it impossible for them to get together this time. "Listen, Bud," John wound up, "let's try for next trip; just give me a call beforehand, and we should be able to arrange things."

Bud got the message; next time, he called ahead. That's when Phase Two of John and Mary's plan went into gear. They wanted the evening to go smoothly, and they wanted to control their time.

When Bud called to announce his arrival, John suggested that they all meet at a particular restaurant. This eliminated the time previously spent at John's house, deciding where to eat and making reservations. It also meant that at the close of the meal, John and Mary were able to say goodnight and head home for a sensible bedtime.

Gradually, Bud and Nancy came to respect the new arrangements. This made it possible to vary the routine. John and Mary knew that they weren't locked into an extended visit every time. They could relax and enjoy hearing all the news from home in ways that had not been possible when they were seething with resentment under their dutiful family smiles.

A bonus for John and Mary was that they felt a lot better about their relatives. By learning how to say "No," they made every "Yes" a sincere one.

## "NO" ISN'T A DIRTY WORD

It's worthwhile to say "No" when you mean "No" because it benefits other people. The most considerate and thoughtful thing you can do for others is to spend time with them because you want to, not because you feel sorry or obligated. Personal relationships built on pity have a rocky road ahead. Compassion for someone in real need is still an important basis for a service relationship. Visiting senior citizens who are hospitalized and have no families, supporting Campfire activities or your local mental health association are certainly healthy and rewarding activities. But personal relationships that are based totally on service are not the best way to fill your social life.

Check it out from your point of view. Would you want

someone to spend time with you because they felt sorry for you or obligated? My hunch is that your answer is an immediate "No." Consider it an absolute minimum of human decency to relate to other people because you want to be with them, not because you feel you "ought to."

Saying "No" also saves you both time and energy. Have you ever said to yourself, "Well, it's only one evening"? Follow up on that idea. There are seven evenings a week; "one evening" is a large percentage of your discretionary time. For people with demanding schedules, it's 100 percent of their available time for the week. Think carefully before using this rationalization for something you don't want to do.

## UNINTENTIONAL RUDENESS

Saying "No" directly is a courtesy to other people. A "No" temporarily wrapped in a "Yes" will crop up in indirect or confusing ways.

Peter and Eileen met each other during coffee break at a seminar. There was an immediate and strong attraction, and for the next few months, they spent every possible minute together. Then Eileen began feeling uncomfortable and closed in, but she didn't tell Peter directly that she needed more time to herself. Instead, she showed her resentment in little' ways—being late, losing things Peter had given her, recognizing more of his weaknesses and pointing them out. When Peter asked her what was wrong, she quickly reassured him, "Everything is fine." But it wasn't. Peter felt confused; Eileen felt trapped. She would have saved them both time and bad feelings by saying "No" directly. If you don't take care of your own needs, you risk inadvertent rudeness to others.

## "YES" AS A BARRIER

Strange as it may seem, sometimes we don't say "No" when we want to because that kind of direct and open communication would open doors to closeness with others. If you spend "obligation" time with someone, it's easy to build up a wall of resentment between the two of you. Some of the most significant and satisfying moments in relationships occur when you give a thoughtful and considerate "No."

## RX FOR SAYING "NO"

Learning how to say "No" when you want to depends on increasing:

- your self-respect
- your confidence about relying on your own standards and decisions
- your comfort about meeting your own needs
- your recognition that you are not responsible for others' feelings
- your understanding that your worth does not depend on other people's judgments
- your comfort and confidence in pleasing yourself.

It's challenging to integrate this prescription into your time program, but each step forward can help you learn when and how to say "No."

*Step 1:* Pick one relationship or type of situation where you've said "Yes" inappropriately several times during the past three or four months. Concentrate on this developmental area first.

*Step 2:* Discover your motivation for saying "Yes." Are you trying to please someone? Are you concerned that "No" might injure the relationship? Are you worried about the other person's feelings?

*Step 3:* Ask yourself when the problem is likely to recur. Is it associated with the weekend? With holidays? With a particular time of day?

*Step 4:* Put together a plan of action for preventing this next time. Part of this step involves preparing yourself for the occasion. Another part involves preventing the occasion from recurring.

In terms of preparation, you may need to remind yourself several times that your worth does not depend on other people's judgments. Tell yourself, "I don't have to please everyone."

In the prevention category, we come back to the idea of directness. If someone asks you out and you do not plan to accept the invitation, it's both fair and thoughtful to let that person know that in some way. Here is what one woman did.

The third time Debra M. was asked out by a colleague she liked but did not want to date, she decided to be more specific.

"George, it means a lot to me to have such a great colleague to work with. I want our good working relationship to continue. I appreciate your asking me to go dancing, but dating isn't what I want. Let's keep what we have. It's a valuable friendship."

*Step 5:* Practice your new response. Get in touch with how you sound and feel as you say "No" in a skillful and thoughtful way. Practice with someone who has good judgment and isn't involved in the situation. You'll be delighted by the ease with which the right words will come to your lips when you've invested the time in practicing. It may not feel "natural" at first, but it will feel natural with practice.

Your personal integrity and worth do not depend on pleasing everyone. These qualities are enhanced by pleasing yourself. Use your time in a way that enables you to say without question, "I did what was right for me. Other people may be doing things I disagree with, but I'm only responsible for me."

Some people may choose to feel hurt no matter what you do. Taking the time to understand and accept your own standards is comforting when you run into someone who wants you to feel guilty. Listen for signals of approaching guilt. When someone says, "If it weren't for you, I . . . ," it's often the envelope that bears an invitation for guilt. Recognize these early warning signals and quickly decline invitations of unrealistic guilt.

## PARENTS AND CHILDREN

It's a real challenge to know when and how to say "No" to the people close to you. It's easy to feel guilty when a parent complains, "But you never call me!" or a child says, "If you really loved me, you'd get it for me." To find the best solution for everyone involved, get some perspective on what they really want from you. For parents and children alike, it's most often simply a need to have you reaffirm your love and affection for them.

Think how easy it would be to give that kind of affirmation to your parents in brief but frequent phone calls. You could sandwich calls in once a week while you're preparing dinner, having a drink after work, before you settle down to read for the evening, or early in the morning, before you go to work. A warm, "Hi Mom, just called to say I love you and am thinking about you," can work wonders. "Dad, I thought of you today when I saw the sunrise; I'm so glad to be your son," is a way to tell your father that you love and honor him. The same principle will work with children. Marilyn C., a working single parent, reported that she spent less time fussing about a "No" with her four and six year olds when she made one of her central daily activities telling each child individually, "I love you." Take the time to do what is important. You'll have a better basis for saying "No" when you need to.

## YOU WANT/I WANT—MIX AND MATCH

*Always* know what you want before you decide to say "Yes." You won't always be able to do what you want or get what you want. But you will make better decisions and take more considerate action if you have this information before you make your decision. Don't stop yourself from knowing what you want by saying things like "I could never do that," or, "It just wouldn't be right."

Clarifying what other people really want can save you time and energy, and still enable them to get everything they want.

Maria was active in her volunteer youth group. She did it because she wanted to, but she dreaded the annual mint sale. All the leaders were expected to open up their car trunks, stack in thirty or forty cases of mints, and sell them. She had wanted to say "No" for the last two years, but felt obligated because it was such a good cause. This year, when the mint sale drive opened, she realized that the organization really wanted a contribution to their budget. She found out how much profit each box brought in, then wrote a check for the amount her allotment of mints would have contributed to the association.

Another member of the executive board used a different tactic. The group did not necessarily expect board members to sell the mints; they just wanted the money for the association. So he gave his trunkload full of mints to a nephew who worked in a tennis club, and the forty cases of mints were sold in a record two days. *Clarify what people want, know what you want, and explore creative ways of achieving both.*

Do not allow yourself to fall into the pit of "feeling obligated" for a favor from a friend. *Assume that other people do things for you because they want to.* If you have potential problems in this area, clarify your stance immediately. Say something like, "Mary, I know you are doing a great deal for me. I appreciate it. It's important for me to know that you aren't doing anything because of a sense of obligation. Only do it if you want to." When you have this kind of understanding, you won't drag yourself down with obligation.

Stop saying "Yes" to people because you believe a "No" will hurt their feelings. Contrary to what you may feel, this isn't thoughtful. In reality, it means that you don't think they have enough personal integrity, strength, and intelligence to manage their own lives. Considered in perspective, it's almost as though your told them, "You poor, weak thing. I know you can't take care of yourself. Even if I don't really want to, I will take on the burden of caring for you because I feel sorry for you." Not very flattering, is it? Essentially, not very thoughtful, either. Give people the same respect you want them to give you. Most want to stand on their own two feet and face life directly. Help them by developing these techniques for saying "No." It will pay off for you both. You'll get even more from your time with people when you:

- Plan ways to prevent the unwilling "Yes."
- Prepare yourself to say "No" with courtesy and skill.
- Practice your responses ahead of time.
- Say "Yes" when it helps others get what they want *and* helps you get what you want.

# 32

## GIVE YOURSELF THE GIFT OF TIME

---

When you shift your daily focus from merely doing what is good (but still secondary) to doing what is the best (the truly central and essential), you reap rich rewards. You move beyond saving time to making time. You gain in confidence. You feel a deep sense of satisfaction. You clarify priorities and develop your judgment of what is temporary and what is really timeless. You enjoy the rewards of quality time.

You now know that you can go beyond the limits of traditional time management and enter the sphere of self-motivation for satisfying and productive action. You probably already have experienced the thrill and exhilaration of implementing some of the techniques discussed in this book. But the pleasure of successful time management isn't an overnight sensation—and it's much more than a mere body of information. Time management is a valuable *skill*. And the psychological principle behind developing this skill is *repetition*.

Don't close the covers of this book and put it away on the shelf. Use it as a constant reference; it's a worthwhile tool and a trustworthy friend. Re-read the chapters that hit closest to home. Talk about them with the special people in your life. Review the techniques that apply to your developmental areas. Turn to this book whenever you want to—you can rely on it as a source of help again and again. In addition, use it to help you feel great about what you have already learned and mastered.

Don't wait for a better day to manage your time effectively. The best is now. Use each day as an opportunity to sort through pressures and demands. Design a pleasing flow of meaningful activities for yourself. Each day, dedicate yourself to the quality lifestyle and accomplishments you want. You deserve them. Go after them.

Throughout this book, I've talked about how important it is for you to know what you want. Now it's my turn to tell you what I want for you.

- I want you to breathe deeply and live this moment fully.
- I want you to achieve your objectives and savor your successes.
- I want you to experience the joyful realization that you deserve to live life to the fullest just because you want to.
- I want you to open yourself to enjoy all the special richness and beauty of this day—to enjoy both your "time in" and your restful "time out."
- I want you to have the sense of peace, purpose and power that comes with being able to say to yourself as you go to sleep, "I took my gift of time today, and I invested it in what really counts. I did what matters most."

Time is a gift. It's always at your fingertips, always ready to be embraced and enjoyed. So greet this day with the eager delight you feel when someone who loves you places a gift in your hands. Accept it joyfully. Appreciate its specialness. Treat it with care. Do your best with this day, and you will give yourself the gift of time.

# REFERENCES AND READINGS

CHAPTER 1. Reaching Beyond Time Management—The
Promise of Quality
Robert F. Mager, *Preparing Instructional Objectives*,
Belmont, California: Fearon Publishers, 1967.

CHAPTER 2. Exposing Myths About Time Management—
Lifting the Veil
Mary McClure Goulding, M.S.W. and Robert L. Gould-
ing, M.D., *Changing Lives Through Redecision
Therapy*, New York: Brunner/Mazel, 1979.

CHAPTER 4. Stimulation, Excitement, Defiance and Your
Time
Eric Berne, M.D., *Transactional Analysis in Psychother-
apy*, New York: Grove Press, Inc., 1961.

Robert L. Goulding, M.D. and Mary McClure Goulding, M.S.W., *The Power Is in the Patient*, San Francisco: TA Press, 1978.

CHAPTER 9. The Five Types of Compulsive Time
Taibi Kahler, Ph.D., with Hedges Capers, Div.M.,
L.H.D., "The Miniscript," in *Transactional Analysis
Journal*, IV, I, January 1974, pp. 26–42.

Taibi Kahler, Ph.D., *Transactional Analysis Revisited*,
Little Rock, Arkansas: Human Development Publica-
tions, 1979.

CHAPTER 11. How To Set Objectives When You Don't
Even Know What You Want
George L. Morrisey, *Management by Objectives and
Results for Business and Industry*, Reading, Massa-
chusetts: Addison-Wesley, 1970.

CHAPTER 12. How to Set Priorities When There's Just Too
Much to Do
Peter F. Drucker, *The Effective Executive*, New York:
Harper & Row, 1979.

8888888888888

CHAPTER 14. Get into Gear and Keep Your System Running Smoothly

Benjamin Franklin, *Autobiography and Other Writings*, L. Jesse Lemisch, Editor, New York: New American Library, 1961.

CHAPTER 17. Procrastination Prevention

Abraham Maslow, *Motivation and Personality*, Second Edition, New York: Harper & Row, 1970.

Abraham Maslow, *Eupsychian Management*, Chicago: Irwin, 1965.

# INDEX

accomplishments, desires for
lifetime, 77, 82, 84–86
accountants, 58
accrued benefits technique,
201–202
action sheet, 127–28
daily. *See* daily action sheet
activity(ies):
analyzing, before diving in,
89–90
grouping related, 101–102,
160, 162
scheduling recurring, 134,
160–61
setting objectives before,
80–81, 82, 92, 173, 178
updating, 83, 85
alarm watch, 176
alternatives, comparing:
to each other, 93, 94, 100
to your objective, 93–96,
100
anxiety, 26
appointments, confirming,
154
attention-getting:
by backed-up paperwork,
172–73
negative stimulation from,
44
by time mismanagement,
19–20, 25, 27
avoidance, 190, 192
of feelings, by procras-
tination, 114–15

balance, 47–48, 192
Be Perfect role, 57–59

techniques for, 59
Be Strong role, 61–62, 71
techniques for, 61–62
big jobs, dividing, into workable steps, 102–103, 147
Bill of Rights, Meeting, 198,
202
blind spots, dealing with,
51–52, 54
boss, the:
five steps to frustration-free
time with, 193–97
discover any unsatisfied
wants, 193–94
know what your boss wants
from you, 195–96
know what you want
*most* from your boss,
194
learn what your boss
wants, 196
treat your boss like a
customer, 196–97
interruptions from, 181–82
marketing to, 197
business expenses, recording
of, on calendar, 107
busyness treadmill, 36
"But I've already taken *the*
time management course
or read *the* book" myth,
13–14
"But there's *nothing* I can do"
myth, 14–15

calculators, 177
calendars, 105–108, 109, 145,
176

choosing, 105–106
departure time, 148–49
getting the most from, 106–107
resistance to using, 107–108
Central Concerns, 84, 85–87, 122, 124, 126
aiming essentials at, 87, 88
doing them first, 88, 101
special papers, 172, 173–74, 176, 178
change, resisting, 23, 25
childhood programming
about time, 42–46, 137, 172
different reactions to same message, 43
listing messages you learned, 44–45
mixed messages, 43–44
negative stimulation, 44
reinforcing the best, 46
sorting out the messages, 42–43
choice time:
potential of, 54
solving the right problems, 55
versus compulsive time, 53–55
differences between, 53
clearing your mind, 125–26, 128
closeness, fear of, 26–27, 170
closing:
of meetings, 200–201
setting time for, 200, 202
of telephone call, 186–87
clothes shopping, 158
"cold turkey" technique, 127–28
commute and travel time, 139–44

assessing travel time, 141
calculating, 141
quarterly checkup, 142–43
complaining about, 140–41, 144
keeping score of daily commute, 139–40
positive use of, 142, 144
preparation time, 142
complaining about commuting, 140–41, 144
compulsive time, 51–66
five types of, 56–66
applying techniques for, 62–63
Be Perfect, 57–59
Be Strong, 61–62, 71
helping others, 63
Hurry Up, 57, 71
Please Me, 59–60
Try Hard, 60–61, 190
key points in conquering, 63
solving the right problems, 55
versus choice time, 53–55
differences between, 53
what is?, 52
what's wrong with, 53
contrast in design, 47–48
control mechanism, misman- agement of time as, 20
creative thinking, special place for, 110

daily action sheet, 108, 109, 142
as aid to others, 109
how to prepare a, 108
to keep up momentum, 109
see also action sheet
daily techniques. See every-

day time demands, strategies to cope with; everyday time management techniques

decisionmaking, speeding up, 92–100
  comparing alternatives to each other, 93, 94, 100
  comparing each alternative with your objective, 93–96, 100
  making fewer decisions, 99
  putting worry in its place, 97
  reviewing what you want, 92–93
  the sequence for, 100
  taking care of yourself, 99
  Timeline Technique, 96–97, 100
  working with odds, not absolutes, 96–97

defiance, 28–33
  creative substitutes for, 30–32
  darker side of, 30
  dealing with those showing, 32–33
  double bind of conflicting motivations, 29–30
  "Just one more thing" ploy, 29
  possible advantage of, 30
  roots of, 28–29

design elements, 47–50
  combining, for your personal style, 49–51

demands, 67, 86–87
  everyday time, 131–66
    commute and travel time, 139–44
    exercise, 163–66
    kicking the lateness

    habit, 145–51
    mornings, 131–38
    reducing waiting time, 152–56
    shopping and housework, 156–62
  organizing in spite of too many, 67–74
    aiming for specifics, 71
    Demands and Interruptions Chart, 68–69, 142
    feeling pressured as its own record, 72
    forecasting demands, 72–73
    keep system simple, 72
    as ongoing process, 74
    preventing and postponing, 73
    sorting-out time, 67–68, 71, 72, 74, 86–87
    starting today, 74
    Time Record and Log, 69–71
  scheduling recurring household, 160–62

Demands and Interruptions Chart, 68–69, 142

departure time, focusing on, 148–49, 151

dividing big jobs, 102–103, 147

doing it your way, 47–50

do it now technique, 104, 110

double bind, 30

early, aiming at being, 146, 151

early birds, imitating, 149

early warning signals of procrastination, 115

emergency care for bad case
of procrastination, 125–28
add reinforcements and
rewards, 127, 128
clear your mind, 125–26,
128
"cold turkey" technique,
127–28
update your wants, 126,
128
engineers, 58–59
equipment, 105–10
to aid paperwork, 177
calendars, 105–108, 109
daily action sheets, 108,
109, 142
special place for creative
thinking, 110
Essentials, 84, 86, 87, 122,
124, 126, 121, 136–37
aiming, at central concerns,
87, 88
doing them first, 88, 102
in the morning, 132–33,
138
recurring, scheduling, 134
special papers, 172, 173,
174, 176, 178
see also Central Concerns
everyday time demands,
strategies to cope with,
131–66
commute and travel time,
139–44
exercise, 163–66
the lateness habit, 149–51
mornings, 131–38
reducing waiting time,
152–56
shopping and housework,
156–62
everyday time management
techniques, 101–104

concentrate on one thing at
a time, 103
divide big jobs into workable steps, 102–103, 147
do central and essential
priorities first, 88, 101
do it now, 104, 110
finish fully, 48, 52, 103–
104, 108, 126, 176, 177
group related activities,
101–102, 160, 162
use a timetable, 103, 162
excitement, stimulation,
defiance, and your time,
26–33, 44, 117–19, 135–
36, 147–48, 151
Excitement and Stimulation
Quota, 26–32, 33, 147, 165
creatively filling your, 30–
32
procrastination prevention
and, 117–18, 119, 124
Procrastination Profile
and, 113–14
executive secretaries, 175
exercise, 163–66
best time for you, 165–66
checking with physician,
164
evaluation, 165–66
implementation, 164
as ongoing program, 164
with others, 165
planning, 163–64
self-motivation through
reward, 164–65

factor sheet, 125, 127
failure, fear of, 97
fear:
of closeness, 24–25, 170
of change, 23, 25
of failure, 97

of feeling "too good," 23–24, 170, 191
of new feelings, 21–22, 25
of overorganization, 16
of success, 170, 171, 190, 191
avoiding, by procrastination, 114–15, 149–50
fear of, 21–25, 170–72, 191
of obligation, 209
finishing fully technique, 48, 52, 103–104, 108, 122, 176, 177–78
flexibility, 49, 50, 83, 109, 136–37,
forecasting demands, 73

gift of time, 211–12
goal setting. *See* objectives, setting
grouping related activities, 101–102, 160, 162
guilt trap, 34–41, 170–71
avoiding, 34, 208
doing what's most important to you, 38–41
how to spot phony guilt, 34–35
"I should be doing better" syndrome, 37–38
perfection syndrome, 38–37, 173
portable guilt, 136
Puritan work ethic, 35–36
springing the, 38–41
treadmill of busyness, 36

harmony of design, 48
housework:
grouping related activities, 160, 162
scheduling recurring demands, 160–61

special projects, 161–62
enlisting aid of partner, 161–62
making sure it's worthwhile, 161
naming, 162
professional help, 157–58, 162
unrealistic standards, 162
*see also* shopping
Hurry-Up role, 59, 71
techniques for, 59

"I always lose my list" myth, 12–13
"I'm waiting until I have more time" myth, 11–12
"I need someone to motivate me" myth, 16
insomnia, 99–100
interruptions, 15, 67, 179–82, 184, 185
Demand and Interruptions Chart, 68–69
direct approach to dealing with, 180–82, 186
some tactful methods, 181
from your boss, 181–82
inconsiderate or just unaware?, 179–80
respect your own time, 182
*see also* demands
"I should be doing better" syndrome, 37–38
"Isn't there a danger you'll get so organized you can't get anything done?" myth, 16
"It doesn't work for me" myth, 12–13

"just in case" papers, 178

"just one more thing" ploy, 29

Kahler, Taibi, 56

last-minute rush, excitement of, 26
late-arrivals, 19–20, 25
  see also lateness habit, kicking the
lateness habit, kicking the, 145–51
  aiming for being early, 146, 151
  combining the techniques, 149, 151
  departure time, 148–49, 150
  early excitement, 147–48, 150
  imitating the early birds, 150
  picking focus points, 145–46
  reasons behind lateness, 150
  rewards and reinforcements, 147, 148
  working backwards, 146–47, 151
  see also late-arrivals
lawyers, 58
librarians, 173, 175
lifestyle, desires for long-term, 77, 82, 84–85
list-losing, 12–13, 108
long-term objectives, 76, 78
  for accomplishments, 77, 82, 84–85
  for lifestyle, 77, 81–82, 84–85
  one hundredth birthday technique, 78

mailing lists, getting off, 173
management consultants, 175
Marginal Matters, 83–84, 88
  paperwork, 176
Maslow, Abraham, 119, 120
meeting(s), 198–202
  Bill of Rights, 198, 202
  clarifying objectives in advance, 198–99, 202
  clueing with questions, 199–200
  collecting accrued benefits, 201–202
  specifying what's expected, 200, 202
  stating the closing time, 200, 202
  wrapping up, 200–201, 202
messy desk myth, 172
mismanagement of time, secret pleasures of, 18–25, 72, 131, 150–51
  as attention-getter, 19–20, 25, 27
  to avoid closeness, 24, 170
  to avoid new feelings, 21–22, 25
  to avoid responsibility, 21–22
  as control mechanism, 20, 25
  fear of feeling "too good," 23–24, 170, 191
  to resist change, 23, 25
  to sidestep the unpleasant, 20–21
  see also lateness habit, kicking the
mistakes, fear of making, 97
mornings, 132–43
  building around essentials, 132–33, 136–37, 138
  comforts of chaos, 137

flexibility, 136–37
ideal, fantasy of, 132
night-before planning, 134–35, 137
preparing for the unexpected, 133–34
pre-sleep suggestion, 133
scheduling recurring activities, 134, 137
stimulation to get going, 135–36
teaming-up for good, 137
"time in" and "time out," 131–32, 137
motivation(s), 6, 119
avoidance as, 190
double bind of conflicting, 29–30
information and, 4–5
myth about, 16, 119
*see also* self-motivation
myth of messy desk, 172
myths about time management, 6, 11–17
"But I've already taken *the* time management course or read *the* book," 13–14
"But there's *nothing* I can do," 14–15
clearing out old, 16–17
"I always lose my list," 12–13
"I'm waiting until I have more time," 11–12
"I need someone to motivate me," 16–17
"Isn't there a danger you'll get so organized you can't get anything done?," 114
"It doesn't work for me," 12–13

"People keep interrupting me," 15
"Time management is boring," 15
"You can't get organized around here," 14

naming special projects, 162
new feelings, avoiding, 21–22, 25
night-before planning, 134–35, 137
"No," saying, 203–10
benefits of, 205–206
to relatives, 204–11
parents and children, 208–209
Rx for, 207–208
unintentional rudeness, 206
"yes" as a barrier, 206–207
you want/I want, 209–10

objectives, setting, 75–82
in advance of meetings, 198–99, 202
commute and travel time and, 139–40
decisionmaking and, 93–95, 99
keeping activities up to date, 81–82, 85
objectives before activities, 80–81, 92–93, 173, 178
one hundredth birthday technique, 78
periodic updating, 80, 81–82, 84–85
security of short-term, 78–79
steps for, 82
two big questions, 76–77
Wants Inventory, 75–76, 85, 86

"What-I-Want-to-Happen"
memo, 79–80
yardstick for, 81–82
obligation, feelings of, 209–
10
one hundredth birthday technique, 77–78
one thing at a time, doing,
103
on-the-job time management,
6
five steps to frustration-
free time with your boss,
193–97
interruptions, 179–82
meeting time, 198–202
paperwork, 169–78
the telephone, 183–87
workaholics, 188–92
see also specific time management techniques
order, 47
organizing yourself, 67–110
overorganization, fear of,
15–16

paperwork, 169–78
daily success strategy,
175–76
determining best method
for response, 177–78
equipment to aid, 176–77
focusing and finishing, 176
getting off mailing lists, 173
getting outside help with,
175
"just in case" papers, 173–
74, 178
key word outline to answer
letters, 177–78
myth of the messy desk,
172
psychological reasons for

problems with, 170–72
quiz on, 169–70
retention schedules, 174
special place technique,
174, 175, 176, 178
special time for, 174–75
starting by uncovering
special papers, 172–73,
175
Pareto, Vilfredo, 88–89, 172
parties, how to end your,
155–56
"People keep interrupting
me" myth, 15
perfection syndrome, 36–37,
173
see also Be Perfect role
personal style of time management, 47–50
classic elements of design,
47–50
right recipe for each
occasion, 48–49
physical fitness. See exercise
Please Me role, 59–60
techniques for, 60
postponing demands, 73–74
pre-sleep suggestion, 133
pressures, overcoming, 6
travel time, 142
see also demands, inter-
ruptions
preventing demands, 73
prevention procrastination.
See procrastination,
prevention
priorities, how to set, 83–91
analyzing activities before
diving in, 89–90
Central Concerns, 84, 86–
87, 88, 101
aiming essentials, at,
87–88

determining what went
   wrong, 90
80 percent gets an "A," 91
Essentials, 84, 86, 87, 88,
   101
   aiming, at central con-
      cerns, 87–88
   grouping every potential
      time investment, 88
   Marginal Matters, 83–84,
      88
   preparing for the unex-
      pected by knowing,
      133–34
   Secondary Matters, 84–85,
      88
   targeting your time, 83–89
   things worth doing per-
      fectly, 91
   20/80 ratio, 88–89
procrastination, 6, 29, 113–28
   as avoidance measure,
      114–15
   early warning signals, 115
   emergency care for bad
      case of, 125–28
      add reinforcements and
         rewards, 126–27
      clear your mind, 125–26
      "cold turkey" technique,
         127–28
      update your wants, 126
   how you handle, 114
   prevention, 117–24
      by getting sufficient
         stimulation, 117–18,
         124
      how approach works for
         some people, 121–22
      how to make approach
         work for you, 121–22
      as justified activity,
         123–24

   new approach to moti-
      vation, 120
   rewarding and reinforc-
      ing the best, 122–23
   self-motivation and un-
      satisfied needs, 119–22
   by substitution of posi-
      tive stimulation for
      negative, 118–19, 124
   three keys to, 117
   three R's of, 122, 124
   profile. *See* Procrastination
      Profile
   the when of, 115
   *see also* mismanagement of
      time, secret pleasures of;
      motivation(s)
Procrastination Profile, 113–
   16
   charting your, 115–16
   early warning signals, 115
   how you handle procras-
      tination, 114
   knowing what you're
      avoiding, 114–15
   Stimulation and Excite-
      ment Quota and, 113–14
   the when of procrastina-
      tion, 115
professional shoppers, 157–
   58, 162
psychology of time, 5–6, 11–
   63

quiz on paperwork, 169–70

recording devices, telephone,
   187
reinforcements, positive,
   122–23, 124, 127, 128
   for being early, 147, 148
relatives, saying "no" to,
   204–205

parents and children, 208–209
repetition in procrastination prevention, 122, 124
responsibility, shirking, 22–23
rewards, 122, 123, 124, 127, 128
for being early, 147, 148
for exercising, 164–65
room for creative thinking, 110

satisfied needs, 119–20
see also unsatisfied needs
scheduling activities:
on personal calendar, 107
recurring essentials, 134, 138
recurring household demands, 160–61, 162
shopping, 158
scientists, 58–59
Secondary Matters, 84–86, 88, 89
paperwork, 176
self-employed as workaholic, 191–92
self-motivation, 113–28
emergency care for bad case of procrastination, 125–28
exercise and, 164–65
procrastination prevention, 117–24
three keys to, 117
satisfied needs and, 119–20
unsatisfied needs and, 120–22
your procrastination profile, 113–16
charting, 115–16
see also motivation(s)
seven classic techniques for

everyday success, 101–104
shopping:
for clothing, 158
grouping related items, 159
professional help, 157–58, 162
schedule, 158
special shopping list, 159–60
standard shopping list, 158–59, 160
for staples in quantity, 159, 160
at stores that deliver, 158
short-term objectives, 76, 79, 82
sorting-out time, 67–68, 71, 72, 74, 86
special place technique for paperwork, 174, 175, 176, 178
Stimulation and Excitement Quota, 26–32, 33, 147, 165
creatively filling your, 31–32
Procrastination Profile and, 113–14
procrastination prevention and, 117–18, 119, 124
stimulation, excitement, defiance, and your time, 26–33, 44, 117–19, 135–36, 147–48, 150
see also Stimulation and Excitement Quota
stress, 26–27, 165, 166
success:
fear of, 170, 171, 190, 191
long hours and, 190–91
savoring, 191
suffering and effective time use, 5

tape recorders, 177
targeting your time, 83–88
team approach:
  for good mornings, 137
  for meetings, 198
techniques for time management:
  choosing the best for you, 52, 56
  for everyday success, seven classic, 101–104
  *see also* specific techniques
telephone, 110, 183–87
  being considerate of others, 185–86, 187
  closing the call, 186–87
  controlling the conversation, 186, 187
  determining what you want to accomplish, 184–85
  discovering where your time is going, 183–84
  interruptions, 181, 184, 185
  people come first, 187–88
  recording devices, 187
  spotting recurring problems, 185
  "unplugging," 187
Timeline Technique, 96–97, 100
"Time management is boring" myth, 15
time management program:
  five steps to, 6–7
  how to use this book, 7–8
  information and motivation, 4–5
  lack of rigidity in, 3–4
  themes of this book, 6
  therapeutic approach of, 5–6
  why it works, 2–3
  *see also* specific phases of program and time management techniques
Time Record and Log, 69–71
timetable, using a, 103, 162
"to-do" list. *See* daily action sheet
travel time. *See* commute and travel time
Try Hard role, 60–61, 190
  techniques for, 61
20/80 rule, 88–89, 172–73
"two-for-the-price-of-one" technique, 201–202

unity of design, 48
unpleasant chores, putting off, 20–21
unsatisfied needs, 120–22, 124
  *see also* satisfied needs
unsatisfied wants, 193–94

vital ingredients, identifying, 88–89
  by determining what went wrong, 90

waiting for others, 32–33, 54–58
  fighting back, 153–55
    arming yourself against waiting, 153–54
    eliminating what you can, 154
    making the best of the rest, 155
  how to end your parties, 155–56
  winning the twenty-fifth hour, 156

wants:
  commute and travel time
    and, 139–40
  unsatisfied, 193–94
  updating your, 126, 127,
    128, 197
Wants Inventory, 75–76, 82,
  85, 86
wardrobe consultant, 158
warning signals of procrastination, early, 115
watches, alarm, 176
"What-I-Want-to-Happen"
  memo, 79–80
workaholic, are you a?, 188–
  92
  avoidance as motivation,
    190, 192
  balance of work, play, and
    love, 192
  doing and being, distinction
    between, 192
fear of feeling good, 191
  long hours and success,
    190–91
  self-employed, 191–92

savoring success, 191
  ten key questions, 188–89
working backwards tech-
  nique, 140–47, 151
worry:
  getting the right perspective
    on, 97–98
  scheduling your, 98–99

yardstick for designing objectives, 81
"yes" when you want to say
  "no," saying, 203–10
  benefits of saying "no,"
    205–206
  to relatives, 204–205
    parents and children,
      208–209
  Rx for saying "no," 207–
    208
  unintentional rudeness, 206
  "yes" as a barrier, 206–207
  you want/I want, 209–10
"You can't get organized
  around here" myth, 14

## SIGNET Books of Special Interest